THE WORLD'S COOLEST HOTEL ROOMS

HarperCollins books may be purchased
for educational, business, or sales
promotional use. For information, please
write: Special Markets Department,
HarperCollins*Publishers*, 10 East 53rd
Street, New York, NY 10022.

First published in 2008 by:
Collins Design
An *Imprint of*
HarperCollins*Publishers*
10 East 53rd Street
New York, NY 10022
Tel: (212) 207-7000
Fax: (212) 207-7654
collinsdesign@harpercollins.com
www.harpercollins.com

Distributed throughout
the world by:
HarperCollins*Publishers*
10 East 53rd Street
New York, NY 10022
Fax: (212) 207-7654

Library of Congress
Control Number: 2007942789

ISBN: 978-0-06-135386-4

Book Design by War Design
www.wardesign.com.au

Printed in China

First Printing, 2008

COLLINS|DESIGN

An Imprint of HarperCollins*Publishers*

THE WORLD'S COOLEST HOTEL ROOMS

Bill Tikos

EUROPE

Global in scope, *The Cool Hunter Guide: The World's Coolest Hotel Rooms* is the result of personal research and travel in pursuit of the coolest of the cool in design, architecture, fashion, technology, and culture. While tracking down the best tube station art in London or the newest karaoke bars in Japan or the most cutting-edge wine cellars in France, I've been lucky enough to stay in some of the world's most unique hotel rooms, too.

It's difficult to say what makes one thing cool and another thing a throwaway. My observations and predictions of new or existing cultural trends are largely based on gut-level instincts. When I find something authentically cool, I know it the moment I see it. The reaction is that instant, something like the "wow" factor; it's being able to have my finger on the pulse at exactly the right moment. A good friend of mine, a trusted fashion analyst and cool hunter in his own right, uses the expression "Streets is hot," when he spots something particularly off-the-grid original. What he means is that there's a movement behind the trend; it's reached its breaking point. There aren't just one or two people who have caught on but, rather, a whole group who are ready to pounce on it and fill the streets. My goal is to get there before everyone else does and recognize the trend at its source, sometimes in the very moment when it is still forming.

This is not to say that all of the hotels featured in this book are new. Yes, some are just-opened boutiques while others are part of established chains or long-running family-run operations. What connects these rooms to each other—what makes them cool—is that, in their individual way, they've bucked the system. These are not your average hotel rooms with basic beds, TV, and bad wallpaper. That bland uniformity of eras past is over, and the people leading the revolution are some of the world's savviest designers, decorators, and architects: people with a definitive sense of vision and possibility. True trendsetters.

The goal here is not to compartmentalize but to identify certain gradations of hipness that come into play within every category. What makes an eco-friendly room cool, for example, is not the same thing that makes a $5,000-a-night luxury penthouse suite cool. For each entry, I've provided a spot-on observation as to what makes each room worth the trek. The rooms presented here were chosen for their forward-thinking approach to design and timeless appeal. Fashion is always in style if it's good and, believe me, there are no flash-in-the-pans here.

In order to stay ahead of the shifts in style, I'm always on the move, which is a good thing since I'm not the type of person who sits still for long. After all, there are new cities to discover, contacts to make, and trends to discover. My yearning for the authentic guides every selection I make in determining what is cool, and I'm positive that these rooms fit the bill.

Roaming the globe, so you're in the know.
–Bill Tikos

AFR

RICA

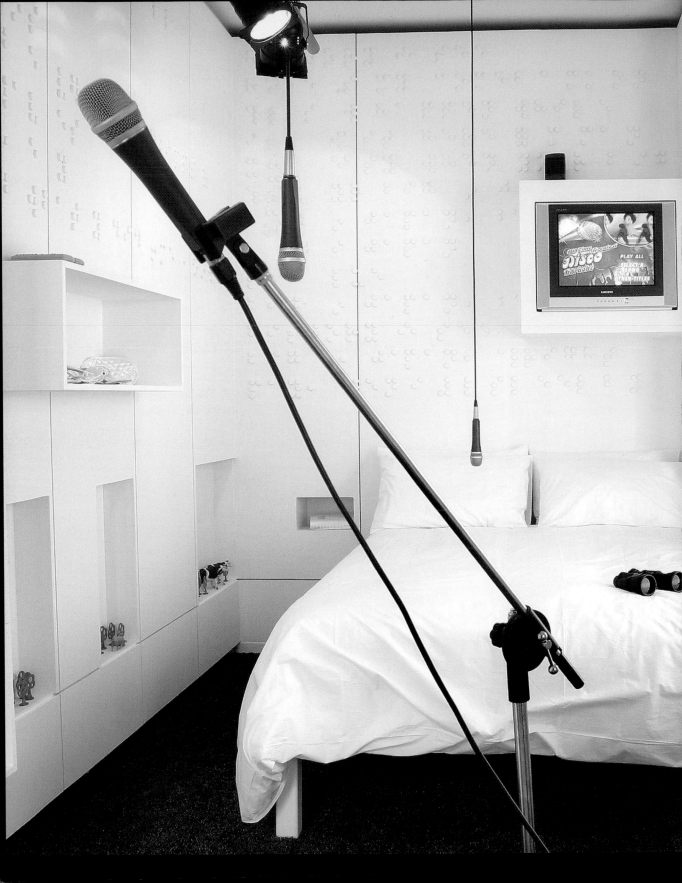

Location
**Cape Town,
South Africa**
Room
Please Do Not Disturb
Architect
Scott Johnston
Designer
Kim Stern
Rate
Inexpensive

THE INNOVATIVE,
CUTTING-EDGE ROOMS
REFLECT THE CREATIVITY
OF CAPE TOWN'S MOST
INGENIOUS ARTISTS.

DADDY
LONG LEGS

A PORTION OF
EACH ROOM'S RATE
IS DONATED TO CHARITY.
THE EMERGENCY ROOM
SUPPORTS A CHILDREN'S
HOSPITAL.

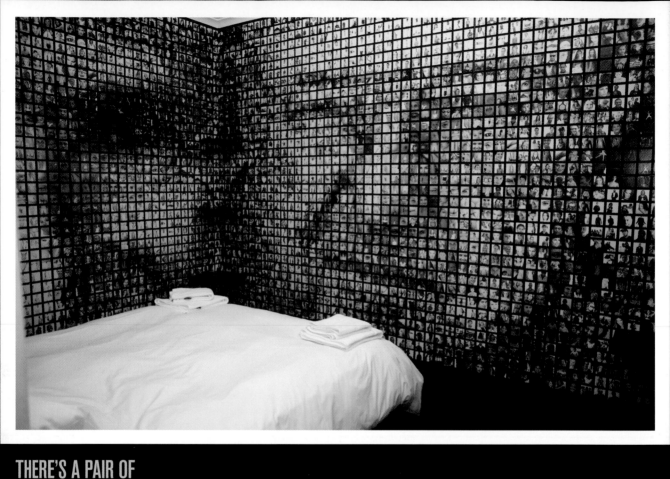

THERE'S A PAIR OF
SUPERSIZED BINOCULARS
IN THE PHOTO BOOTH
ROOM SO GUESTS CAN
AMUSE THEMSELVES WITH
A DETAILED VIEW OF CAPE
TOWN'S NIGHTLIFE.

The cosmopolitan city of Cape Town plays host to one of the world's most innovative artist-designed boutique hotels. Situated on Long Street—the heart and soul of this South African city—Daddy Long Legs boasts 13 individually designed and themed rooms. From the sleek and polished look of the Protea Room (page 12), furnished with a dark black lacquer interiors, to the whimsically designed Photo Booth Room (left), decorated with 3,240 portraits of Cape Town residents, Daddy Long Legs has something for everyone, even those with the most discerning or eclectic taste.

Staying at the hotel is like spending the night in an interactive art exhibition and the best example of that is room 13, Please Do Not Disturb (pages 10 to 11), designed by local artist/curator Kim Stern. Part fantasy sound studio/stage and part bedroom, this room allows guests to reinvent themselves as rock stars, if only for a night or two. Complete with a clean retro feel and authentic theatrical lighting, a karaoke machine, and five microphones—one of which is located in the shower—would-be divas can soap up and get down all at the same time. The walls are reminiscent of soundproof egg-carton insulation and are decorated with the lyrics from Alphaville's "Big in Japan." Tucked inside the nightstand is the ubiquitous Bible, but done up in mod-style padded white leather. And if this doesn't garner interest, supersized binoculars afford visitors a detailed view of the surrounding cityscape, especially brilliant and full of life at night. Astroturf carpeting, an orange telephone, and a stainless steel washbasin round out this fantastically designed music studio-cum-hotel room.

Whether guests take their song cues from Alphaville or find inspiration from the collection of local South African music offered at the African Music Store, which is located street level to the hotel, Please Do Not Disturb promises to embellish every musical fantasy. With a selection of satin sleep masks to choose from, each one embroidered with a girl's name, guests will dream like a rock star, too. More a gallery than a hotel, Daddy Long Legs and its team of 13 artists have brought humor and endless creativity to hotel décor.

Special feature
A percentage of the room's rate is donated to a specific charity. The Emergency Room (page 13), for example, supports the Red Cross Children's Hospital.

Can't miss
The colorful graffiti mural by the celebrated South African graffiti artist Faith is located just outside the windows of Please Do Not Disturb.

Daddy Long Legs
134 Long Street
Cape Town, South Africa
T 27 (0) 21 424 1403
F 27 21 422 3446
www.daddylonglegs.co.za
info@daddylonglegs.co.za

AMER

RICAS

Location
**Buenos Aires,
Argentina**
Room
Faena Suite
Design/Designer
**Alan Faena and
Philippe Starck**
Rate
Expensive

ONE-PART RENAISSANCE AND ONE-PART *VELVET GOLDMINE*, THE FAENA IS LUXURIOUS WITHOUT BEING GAUDY.

FAENA HOTEL +UNIVERSE

Known as the Paris of South America, Buenos Aires has long enchanted visitors with its European sophistication and Latin charm. So it should come as no surprise that French design maverick Philippe Starck chose the city as the site for his most daring design statement yet: The Faena Hotel + Universe. Working in collaboration with owner Alan Faena, Starck combines a belle époque aesthetic with modern elegance.

The experience of transformation begins with the main entrance lobby (page 21, lower right), called the Cathedral and for good reason. Gold velvet curtains run the length of floor-to-ceiling windows, which are etched in red-stained glass. The long central pathway, adorned with red carpet and black-and-gold benches, is impressive and sets the tone for the rooms that follow. Formerly a historic grain building, Faena contains 110 guest rooms, along with 83 permanent residences.

The large Faena Suite (pages 18 to 19, library; page 21, left, bedroom) is by far the most sumptuous of all the rooms. As the most expensive suite in all of Latin America, it is a must for those seeking decadence and style. Located on the building's top floors, this two-story suite features striking views of the Puerto Madero canal and the surrounding cityscape. The suite boasts such amenities as 18-carat gold leaf swan chairs, Tuscan marble baths, and a private sunset terrace. A fully equipped kitchen with service entrance and an imperial-themed dining room—with seating for ten—offers the ultimate environment for upscale entertaining. The master bathroom includes a walk-in shower, a Jacuzzi built for two, and a baroque-styled sink (page 21, upper right). Deep red velvet curtains are offset by dark lapacho wood flooring, accented with light paloma sandstone. Hand-chosen antique collectibles add a distinctly personal touch. With guests like John Galliano and Lenny Kravitz, it's no wonder that the Faena has long-lasting star appeal.

Special feature
An "experience manager." The experience manager is equal parts concierge, butler, and personal assistant. From scheduling an impromptu tango class with the area's leading dancer or chartering a private yacht for a birthday party to simply picking up the dry cleaning, the experience manager elevates the Faena into a class all of its own (although other hotels are quickly following suit).

Can't miss
The complimentary jet-lag massage upon arrival.

Faena Hotel + Universe
Martha Salotti 445
C1107CMB Buenos Aires, Argentina
T 54 11 4010 9000
F 54 11 4010 9001
www.faenahotelanduniverse.com
info@faenaexperience.com

IT'S THE MOST EXPENSIVE
SUITE IN ALL OF SOUTH
AMERICA AND DECORATED
IN GOLD LEAF AND
TUSCAN MARBLE.

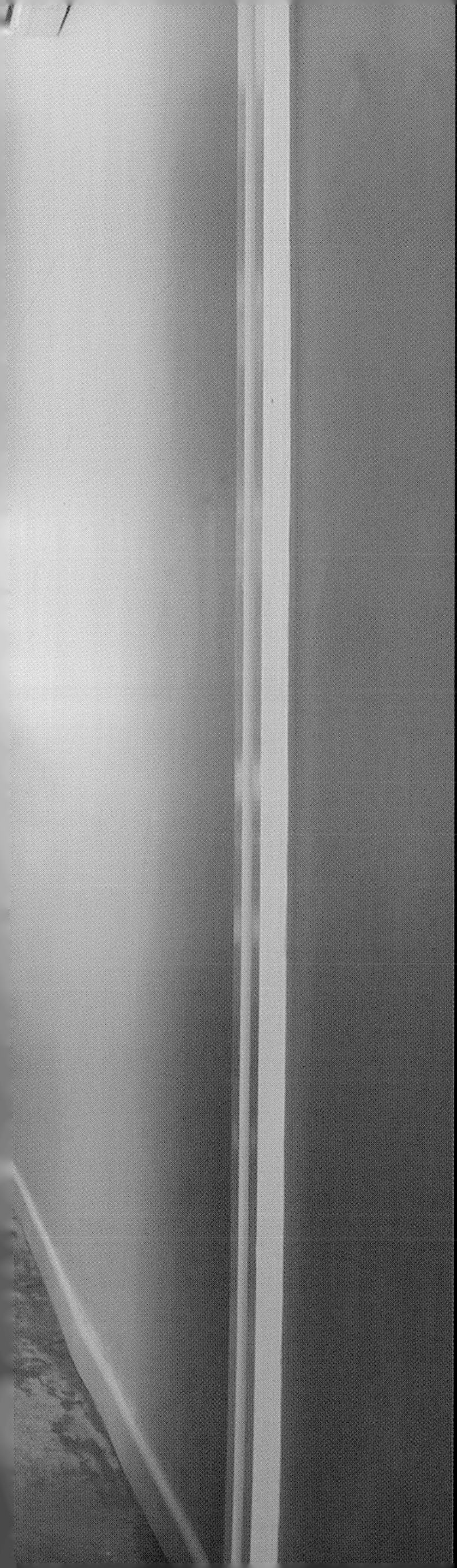

Location
**Buenos Aires,
Argentina**
Room
Garden Suite
Architect
**Rodrigo Cunill
and Juana Grichener**
Designer
**Rodrigo Cunill,
Juana Grichener,
Tom Rixton, and
Patricia O'Shea**
Rate
Expensive

THIS HOTEL OFFERS EASY-GOING, DOWN-HOME APPEAL AND 1960s-STYLE SOPHISTICATION.

HOTEL HOME

THE GARDEN SUITE
COMES COMPLETE
WITH ITS OWN
POOL AND PRIVATE
ROOFTOP TERRACE.

Despite its reputation as a party destination, Buenos Aires, surprisingly, has little in the way of luxury boutique hotels. British record producer Tom Rixton and his PR-savvy wife, Patricia O'Shea, changed that in 2005 with their smartly designed Hotel Home, located in the hip district of Palermo Viejo. Initially the couple realized the lack of stylish hotel digs while planning their own wedding in Buenos Aires. "We wanted our friends and their friends to visit this fantastic neighborhood and city. So we created Home," O'Shea explains. Financed by fellow record producer Flood (who's worked with U2, Nick Cave and the Bad Seeds, and PJ Harvey, among others) and Crowded House bass player Nick Seymour, Home has become a destination spot in its own right, due in large part to the owners' low-key attitude and quirky design sense that mixes vintage Scandinavian furniture with whimsical Parisian wallpaper.

The hotel's designers worked closely with Rixton and O'Shea to create interiors that are light and airy, simple and serene. While all 17 rooms share a streamlined aesthetic, the Garden Suite (pages 22 to 24) combines all the best architectural features of the hotel—polished cement floors, floor-to-ceiling windows, and beautiful hardwood decks—with an element of fun. The furniture is stark white, accented with pillows and tapestries of canary yellow and lime green. The highlight of the suite, however, is its shallow pool. Built as an extension of the hotel's main pool, it continues into the exterior space of the suite and is flanked by tropical plants and several different lounge areas. The private rooftop terrace isn't shabby, either. Dotted with tons of flowers and lemon trees, the terrace offers great views of the hotel's lush garden and turquoise-colored pool. A little-known fact: Those lemons are used for cocktails at the bar. How's that for homegrown?

Special feature
The Garden Suite wallpaper was first seen in a 1967 issue of *Elle Décor.*

Can't miss
The rosemary-and-sorrel vodka martinis. The expert bartender serves them strong at the outdoor bar, where there's plenty of room for dancing around the pool and garden to the music spun by the house DJ.

Hotel Home
Honduras 5860
Buenos Aires, Argentina
T 54 11 4778 1008
www.homebuenosaires.com/home
info@homebuenosaires.com

Location
**Montreal,
Canada**
Room
Black Suite
Architect
**In Situ Design,
New York**
Designer
**Acanto Interiors
and Ana Barrallo**
Rate
Moderate

URBANE, COOL, AND
MODERN, THE ST. PAUL
ELEVATES MINIMAL DÉCOR
INTO AN ART FORM.

ST. PAUL
HOTEL

While the St. Paul Hotel's exterior is emblematic of muscular beaux arts architecture (page 29, bottom), its interior favors soft lines, a calming monochromatic design palette, and an airy, almost ethereal atmosphere that reflects the natural beauty of the surrounding Canadian landscape. This juxtaposition of the masculine and the feminine, the old and the new, befits a hotel poised on the edge of the heritage-rich Old Montreal and its hip neighbor, Multimedia City, Montreal's answer to Silicon Valley. The 120 guestrooms reflect one of four design elements: fire, ice, sky, and earth, and create a sense of harmony and tranquility that permeates throughout the entire hotel. Sky-centered rooms contain gauzy white curtains and ample natural light, while earth-centered rooms are rich in beiges, browns, and tactile furnishings (page 29, top).

The only room that strays from this design scheme happens to be the hotel's best: the Black Suite (pages 26 to 27). Located on the penthouse floor, the suite is awash in charcoal black walls and 13-foot high ceilings. A stunning collection of antiques like rare Gio Ponti lamps decorate the room, and the pony-skin chairs are especially dramatic. Four shuttered windows open to reveal the metropolitan skyline, one of the best views in Montreal. The mosaic-tiled bathroom, outfitted with a soaker tub, is the epitome of understated elegance. Marble and raw metal combine with silk and glass to create the signature St. Paul look: classic yet contemporary, minimalist yet sensual. Hardwood floors, a vaulted cathedral-like ceiling, and an original cherry-wood art deco table are among the room's special features. In keeping with the room's dark cocoalike hue is a daily selection of refined, handcrafted chocolates—the perfect accompaniment to chilled champagne.

Special feature
The lobby's ice-hot fireplace (page 29, left). Massive and gorgeous, it is layered in translucent alabaster.

Can't miss
The restaurant. Cube is more like an über-cool lounge than hotel restaurant. Try the braised lamb shank with Japanese artichoke, risotto, and thyme.

St. Paul Hotel
355 rue McGill
Montreal
Quebec H2Y 2E8 Canada
T 514 380 2222
F 514 380 2200
www.hotelstpaul.com
info@hotelstpaul.com

**THE FINISHING TOUCH
TO THIS ROOM? A DAILY
HAND-DELIVERED SELECTION**

Location
**Toronto,
Canada**
Room
Suite (XL)
Architect
3rd UNCLE design
Rate
Moderate

WITH ITS PUNK ROCK ROOTS
FIRMLY ESTABLISHED, THE
DRAKE RETAINS ITS REP AS
THE GENUINE ARTICLE BY
KEEPING THREE STEPS AHEAD
OF GLOBAL TRENDSETTERS.

DRAKE
HOTEL

FROM MICK JAGGER TO
ORLANDO BLOOM, A-LISTERS
ARE ATTRACTED TO THE
DRAKE'S BOHO-CHIC VIBE.

As Toronto's unofficial rec room, the Drake Hotel plays host to a range of stylish clientele and Hollywood A-listers, from Mick Jagger to Orlando Bloom. Located at the center of the once grungy strip of Queen Street West, the Drake retains its status as an iconic forward-thinking mecca of culture, art, and community in large part due to its celeb connections and the bar's 4:00 AM last call. But don't underestimate the power of its bohemian sensibility and authentically artistic approach to interior design; it's enough to woo other converts eager to explore life in the big T.O.

The Drake had its start in the 1890s, but by the 1980s, it was sidelining as a punk bar, all-night rave den, and flophouse. Since then, the Drake has cleaned up a bit, though it still retains its edginess and reputation as a community hangout, complete with rooms called "crash pads" and "dens," a hipster-meets-hippie café, and a rocking underground stage, which fronts local DJs and bands. The décor reflects this laid-back attitude, featuring mismatched vintage furniture and floral wallpaper. The bohemian feel gets a jolt with the Drake's permanent collection of contemporary art, which includes the likes of Evan Penny and Yuh-Shiuh Wong, among others. An on-site curator and artist-in-residence guarantees that the hotel remains at the forefront of global artistic trends and cultural movements.

Special feature
The eclectic arts programming on the in-house Drake television.

Can't miss
The Sky Yard. This Moroccan-inspired, open-air rooftop playground is the hot spot for celeb sightings and cocktails that pack a punch.

Each of the hotel's 19 rooms are unique, with high ceilings, and in some cases, exposed brick walls. For a true dose of healthy decadence, though, snag the hotel's sole suite. Large enough to live up to its name—Suite (XL)—its open floor plan is ingeniously punctuated with vinyl curtains that separate the living room, bedroom, and bathroom (pages 30 to 32). The room's standout feature is its sexy shower. With a direct sight line to the bed, the all-glass stall inspires voyeurism. The lime green carpet is a welcome contrast to the expansive all-black leather couch, making for one cool crash pad, whether or not friends are in tow.

After a night hobnobbing at one of the hotel's five restaurants or three clubs, order in a bit of romance from the hotel's "pleasure service menu." Among the adult offerings: how-to sex manuals, sultry videos, velvet blindfolds, and an assortment of vibrators. As owner Jeff Tober says, "Hotels have always represented opportunities for guests to experiment, fantasize, and improvise, and we are merely a conduit to those aspirations."

From the hotel's artistic ambience to its friendly staff and funky décor, a stay at the Drake always feels like hanging out at a friend's house. It's boho-chic done right.

Drake Hotel
1150 Queen Street West
Toronto, Ontario M6J 1J3 Canada
T 416 531 5042
F 416 531 9493
www.thedrakehotel.ca

Location
Caribbean,
St. Barths
Room
Howard Hughes Suite
Architect
Rémy de Haenen and
David and Jane Matthews
Rate
Expensive

THERE'S A REASON THIS
CARIBBEAN PARADISE
HAS EDEN AS PART OF ITS
MONIKER. ENDLESS SKIES,
SEAS, AND TROPICAL FLAIR
MAKE IT A STANDOUT.

EDEN ROCK

ONCE THE HAUNT OF
ECCENTRIC BILLIONAIRE
HOWARD HUGHES,
EDEN ROCK IS NOW
A PLAYGROUND FOR
JET-SETTERS LIKE
SEAN COMBS.

Like Aspen and St. Tropez, the island of St. Barths is a haven for the rich and famous. For as long as celebrities, heiresses, and moguls have been visiting the white-sand playground, they have been checking into the Eden Rock hotel. Regulars vary from David Letterman to Sean Combs and Paul McCartney to Usher.

The hotel's unique outcrop setting means that guestrooms are either positioned into the island rock or just steps above the water (pages 36 and 37, bottom). Having recently undergone a $25 million renovation, the original rooms enchant with family heirlooms, steamer trunks, four-poster beds, and watercolors of local scenes by co-owner Jane Matthews. The hotel's *pièce de résistance*, however, is the newly constructed Howard Hughes Suite (page 37, top), named after the eccentric businessman and confidant to the hotel's original owner, Rémy de Haenen, a celebrated adventurer and the first mayor of the island.

Perched above the hotel's Main House on the craggy rock, the suite features the best views of the Caribbean by virtue of its three spacious terraces that offer 360-degree views of the beaches, blue water, and surrounding coral (pages 34 to 35). With a sunken bath, handcrafted furniture, private pool and deck, and Jacuzzi®, the suite is an attractive spot for any recluse. The living room's dark angelique-and-ipeh wood floors are offset by two cream-colored couches and cobalt-colored curtains. The suite's bedroom is designed in warm Caribbean shades of turquoise and cumulus-inspired whites; the two bathrooms are clad in welded copper that's oxidized into an emerald-like patina by the salt air.

More the stuff of fairy tales than real life, the Eden Rock Hotel is one of the few places in the world where a visit feels like an exclusive invitation high in glamour and the celebrity quotient. The continual white noise of six-seater planes overhead further solidifies the hotel's reputation as the jet-setter's paradise.

Special feature
On the Rocks (page 39). The hotel's restaurant serves such delectable French-fusion cuisine that celeb-spotting takes a backseat.

Can't miss
Gustavia Harbor. As the island's main dock, this is the place to spot the big players with their very big boats. Ron Perelman's 187-foot yacht *Ultima III* was stationed here.

Eden Rock
St. Jean Bay
St. Barths, 97133
French West Indies
590 590 29 79 94
590 590 29 79 98
www.edenrockhotel.com

THE CUISINE AT THE
RESTAURANT IS SO
DELECTABLE THAT
GUESTS FORGET
TO KEEP AN EYE OUT
FOR THE CELEBS.

Location
**Puerto Natales,
Chile**
Room
Suite Indigo
Architect
Sebastián Irarrázabal
Designer
Ana Ibañez
Rate
Moderate

NOT CONTENT TO RIDE
THE WAVE OF SUSTAINABLE
ARCHITECTURE, INDIGO
IS THE REAL DEAL. THINK
OF IT AS A HOTEL/SPA MEANT
TO SUSTAIN ITS GUESTS.

INDIGO PATAGONIA

A PERFECT WAY TO RELAX
AFTER A DAY SPENT EXPLORING:
SOAKING IN THE HOT TUB
THAT FACES A VIEW OF
THE FJORD AND THE NEARBY
ANDES MOUNTAINS.

In Patagonia, the long summer nights of the Southern Hemisphere break into beautiful sunrises and dissipate into equally brilliant sunsets. The maritime passage of Puerto Natales presents magnificent views of the glacier Balmaceda, the mountains, and the ever-changing sea. Situated near the coast, Indigo Patagonia offers a luxurious haven for relaxation after backpacking, glacier hiking, or kayaking in Chile's world-renowned Torres del Paine National Park.

Indigo Patagonia is a symmetrical, almost dormlike structure that contains 23 guestrooms and six suites on six different levels. Boldly written across its red corrugated-metal façade is the word *Indigo*, so guests know when they've arrived (page 42, bottom left). Everything in the hotel–inside and out–is made from sustainable materials. Soft ramps and an intricate system of staircases, corridors, and bridges connect the street level to the upper-suite levels (page 42, bottom right). Of the six offered, Suite Indigo (page 42, top) is the best of the bunch; the hot tub, which faces the room's big bay windows, gives guests unobstructed views of the fjord and nearby mountains. The décor is simple: beige carpet, lots of natural wood, white concrete walls, a fireplace, and soft lighting. The textures of Patagonia can be found in the delicate bed linens and exquisite blankets of hand-woven wool. The suite also has direct access to the hotel spa, located on the building's top floor right above it.

Adjacent to the hotel is a lounge bar, and Pez Glaciar, the hotel restaurant. Literally translated as Iced Fish, the restaurant specializes in seafood, especially sushi and ceviche; the bar has perfected the pisco sour–Chile's national cocktail.

Located at the tip of Chile, Indigo Patagonia is the beginning of an adventure into the wilderness. With its ingenious design sense, this hotel is worth going to the end of the world for.

Special feature
The spa, the spa, the spa (pages 40 to 41). Complete with three outdoor Jacuzzis, two massage rooms, and a sauna, it has an uninterrupted view of Ultima Esperanza Fjord, guaranteed to turn anyone into a happy camper.

Can't miss
The walks. The Torres del Paine National Park has plenty of trails to satisfy the most intrepid trekker.

Indigo Patagonia
Ladrilleros 105
Puerto Natales, Chile
T 56 61 413609
www.indigopatagonia.com
info@indigopatagonia.com

julio de la cruz

Location
Playa del Carmen, Mexico
Room
Sea View Suite
Architect
Hectar Galvan
Designer
Omelette
Rate
Moderate

BÁSICO DOES BASIC RIGHT.
THIS IS ONE LAID-BACK
HOTEL—JUST THE WAY
A VACATION SHOULD BE.

HOTEL BÁSICO

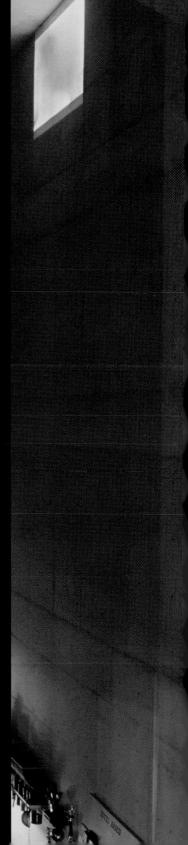

THE HOTEL EXUDES
INDUSTRIAL CHIC;
THE MATERIALS ARE
RECYCLED FROM THE
REGION'S OIL REFINERIES
AND FACTORIES.

As clean, sparse, and simple as its name implies, Básico—the fourth hotel project from the ingenious firm Grupo Habita—elegantly captures the down-to-earth aspects of Mexican culture without sacrificing its glamour, color, or sense of adventure. Both the building's architecture and its interior design utilize distressed retro furnishings and recycled materials from public schools, cantinas, and oil refineries from the 1950s, including tire rubber for furniture and flooring. An old-fashioned and authentically creaky freight elevator is reminiscent of a factory warehouse, while the hotel's exposed pipes, barely varnished wood, and cement floors exude an industrial-chic theme, casual in both its form and function. Two red rooftop swimming pools (page 46, left), modeled after the region's oil tanks, imbue a stripped-down sense of style that extends to the interiors of each of the 15 guestrooms.

Básico has three suites, and of these the most beautiful and refreshingly unpretentious is the Sea View Suite. Here, guests will find an unusually high bed that seemingly floats in the middle of the room, along with an inspiring view of the Caribbean. Designed as a multiuse facility, the bed features integrated drawers, desk space, a minibar, and a safety deposit box. Guest amenities include a beach ball, flippers, and floating tires, all of which are discreetly stowed beneath the bed and serve as a playful reminder that the beach is a short walk away. The shower, sink, and stand-alone bathtub; share the bedroom space (page 49, left); only the toilet is concealed.

With an exterior made out of a mixture of concrete and Caribbean sand (pages 44 to 45), an entrance area modeled after a public market, and an open-air reception area, complete with a desk that functions as an exotic juice-stand by day and a bar by night (page 47), the hotel expertly captures the essence of the beach atmosphere—inside and out. It's the perfect destination for anyone familiar with pairing Proenza Schouler with a T-shirt from American Apparel.

Special feature
The camera. The vintage Polaroid handcuffed to the bed promises documentation of decidedly adult-only proclivities (page 49, right).

Can't miss
The evenings. The hotel comes alive with guest DJs, bottomless mojitos, and video projections of tropical-themed films.

Hotel Básico
5a. Av. and Calle 10 Norte
Playa del Carmen
Quintana Roo, Mexico
T 52 984 879 44 48
F 52 984 879 44 49
www.hotelbasico.com

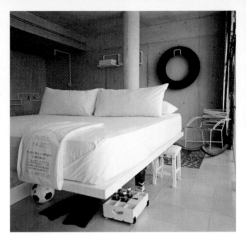

FOR THOSE WHO
WANT TO TAKE BACK
MEMENTOES OF
THEIR STAY, THERE'S
A POLAROID CAMERA
HANDCUFFED TO
THE BED.

Location
**Playa del Carmen,
Mexico**
Room
Ocean View Suite
Architect
Central de Arquitectura
Designer
Omelette
Rate
Moderate

LARGELY UNADORNED,
THE ROOMS AT THIS HOTEL
ARE TRANQUIL ENOUGH TO
SATISFY ANYONE'S DESIRE.

HOTEL
DESEO

A CLOTHESLINE
IS HUNG WITH SUCH
UNEXPECTED GIFTS
AS SUN HATS, BANANAS,
AND AN AMOROUS KIT

Deseo means "desire" in Spanish, and Hotel Deseo fulfills that seductive promise with flowing tapestries, hammocked terraces, and nearby Caribbean beaches with names like Playa del Secreto. This intimate 15-guestroom retreat is located on Playa del Carmen's bustling Avenida Quinta (Fifth Avenue).

The dramatic stone entrance, modeled after a Mayan temple, makes an eye-catching statement with floor-to-ceiling glass panels framed by spindly log balustrades, making it look like a giant Noguchi lamp at night. Though there is no hotel restaurant, the self-service kitchen stocks healthy, complimentary snacks by day and prepares Euro-Latin breakfasts in the morning.

While every room is a cool retreat from the heat with stark white marble floors and a natural color palette, the Ocean View Suite stands alone (page 52). Serenely minimalist with unusual and luxurious touches, including a slide-away bedside table that disappears, incense at turndown, and an array of amenities, this suite offers an unparalleled view of the sugary white beaches and turquoise waters. The sunsets simply can't be beat.

Though secluded, Hotel Deseo hosts an on-going party. The lounge features a multi-decked terrace with king-sized chaises and pillows set around a bar serving drinks and tapas-style snacks. The pool glows purple after dark. Day or night, Deseo draws the young and the hip. The nonstop house music, specially mixed in Paris, and the constant fashion photo shoots are part of the hotel's allure. In fact, it's why Hotel Deseo leads the pack as the best place to see and be seen.

Special feature
The "goodnight kit." In each room, a wire clothesline is strung against a white wall and hung with unexpected amenities, such as woven sun hats, boxer shorts, flip-flops, room service menus, and an amorous kit containing incense and condoms (pages 51 to 52).

Can't miss
The Mayans. Explore the Mayan ruins at Tulum and Coba for a soul-cleansing excursion into archeology.

Hotel Deseo
5a Av. and Calle 12
Playa del Carmen
Quintana Roo, Mexico
T 52 984 879 3620
F 52 984 879 3621
www.hoteldeseo.com
contact@hoteldeseo.com

Location
**Los Angeles,
United States**
Room
Penthouse Suite
Architect
Leland Bryant
Designer
Paul Fortune
Rate
Expensive

AS HOLLYWOOD'S HOME AWAY FROM HOME, THIS HOTEL IS EVERY BIT AS PICTURE-READY AS ONE OF TODAY'S MOST GLAMOROUS INGÉNUES.

SUNSET TOWER HOTEL

Formerly the Argyle, the Sunset Tower is so much a part of Old Hollywood that it is listed in the U.S. National Register of Historic Places. In its heyday as an apartment building with hotel services, the celebrity tenants included John Wayne, Marilyn Monroe, and Frank Sinatra. Reportedly, Howard Hughes lived in the penthouse at one time and owned about 30 apartments where he housed his mistresses.

One of the largest residential art deco buildings in Los Angeles, the exterior is distinguished by continuous columns of windows stretching from top to bottom and cast-concrete friezes depicting a somewhat surreal vision of flora, fauna, airplanes, and zeppelins. When hotelier Jeff Klein took on the renovation of the down-at-the-heels property, he says he brought in designer Paul Fortune to "restore the hotel to what it should be but never was."

While all 74 of the hotel's guestrooms feature high-quality finishes, oversized tubs, and amazing views of the Sunset Strip from the floor-to-ceiling windows, the Penthouse Suite is the hotel's towering achievement (page 54 to 55, and page 57, bottom). It is a luxury apartment, complete with wraparound terraces that offer panoramic views of the Hollywood Hills. The limestone bathrooms feature deep soaking tubs, stand-alone showers, and open-legged vanity consoles with brass fittings (page 57, top).

With its excellent views and terraced pool area, the hotel succeeds in evoking a bygone era of white-glove service and a retreat from the MTV version of glitz. As *Travel and Leisure* puts it, the Sunset Tower is "neither a Hilton, nor a place where you might encounter one."

Special feature
Oldies but goodies. At night, the TerraceLounge softly swings to live piano music or Sinatrarecordings from the 1940s and 1950s.

Can't miss
Hooray for Hollywood. This venture into Hollywood's glamorous and notorious past might be continued with studio tours or by following a map to the homes of the stars.

Sunset Tower Hotel
8358 Sunset Boulevard
Hollywood, CA 90069
T 323 654 7100
www.sunsettowerhotel.com

MARILYN MONROE
CALLED THIS HOTEL
HOME AND HOWARD
HUGHES HOUSED HIS
MISTRESSES HERE.

Location
**Miami,
United States**
Room
Penthouse B
Architect
Charles Benson
Designer
India Mahdavi
Rate
Moderate

ROOMS AT THE TOWNHOUSE
MAY BE DECEPTIVELY
SIMPLE, BUT THE ABSENCE
OF OVER-THE-TOP DÉCOR
IS EXACTLY WHAT MAKES
THE HOTEL DELIGHTFUL.

TOWNHOUSE

THE PENTHOUSE
BALCONY GIVES GUESTS
A BIRD'S-EYE VIEW OF
THE ROOFTOP LOUNGE—
THE HOTTEST PLACE IN
MIAMI FOR PHOTO AND
CASTING SHOOTS.

The Townhouse in Miami's South Beach sizzles with a hip sense of fun and mischief. A half a block from the beach, the 5-story, 70-room hotel glows with a lacquered white "shabby chic" design injected with quirky humor. Free laundry machines in the lobby seem to invite guests to strip down for a quick change of beachwear while they nibble on affordable snacks and beverages, available around the clock. The hotel has a casual vibe that encourages guests to wander the hallways in their pajamas or bathing suits.

The fun continues in Penthouse B, where a beach ball and big baby blue pillows decorate the king-sized bed (pages 58 to 59, and page 60, right). Sexy red-flowered curtains match the old-fashioned fire-engine red telephone in a nod to the building's art deco origins, but the amenities are state of the art, with wireless Internet available everywhere, even on the roof. The room's playful décor and low-key sense of style sets the tone for stress-free R&R. Outfitted with two couches, there is plenty of room to stretch out or entertain. Bathroom amenities include the marble tub, rainfall shower, and complimentary (and comfy) robe and slippers (page 60, left).

The real reason to stay here, though, is for the view. With a balcony overlooking the rooftop lounge, Penthouse B affords a bird's-eye view of the scene below—one of the hottest in Miami. Here, guests lounge under bright red parasols. A giant glow-in-the-dark tower dispels a refreshing mist and the sounds of Miami's latest tunes. A natural draw for casting and photo shoots, the rooftop is a welcome hangout for any entourage. Celebs like Charlize Theron, Chloë Sevigny, and Matt Damon—among countless others—frequent the Townhouse, making it one of the best places to roam the hallways.

Special feature
The queen-sized water beds. The rooftop terrace has plenty of them so guests can lounge in style.

Can't miss
Bond St. lounge. Located on the ground floor, this casual-yet-intimate restaurant is Miami's outpost of the famed New York sushi restaurant.

Townhouse
150 20th Street
Miami Beach, FL 33139
T 305 534 3800
F 877 534 3811
www.townhousehotel.com
info@townhousehotel.com

Location
**Minneapolis,
United States**
Room
Rock Star Suite
Architect
David Rockwell
Rate
Expensive

THE CHAMBERS' ART
COLLECTION RIVALS SOME
OF AMERICA'S MOST
PRESTIGIOUS GALLERIES
AND SETS THE BAR
FOR OTHER HOTELIERS.

CHAMBERS

Unbelievable but true: Minneapolis is white-hot and nothing exemplifies its burgeoning sex appeal than the Chambers. Daring and visionary in form, the hotel rivals the architectural savvy of the Walker Art Center and the Guthrie Theater. It's edgier than its big-city sibling, Manhattan's Chambers, and draws a nightly scene of shock-art bad boys and girls and glammed-up trendsetters.

When property developer Ralph Burnet bought a former flophouse and its adjoining print shop, architect David Rockwell revived the landmark buildings into a hotel and showcase for Burnet's private collection of contemporary art, including many works by British artists like Damien Hirst and Gary Hume. The hotel's corridors are lined with Damien Hirst's pill-popping charts from his *Last Supper* series, and his desiccated Judas Iscariot bull's head looms behind the reception desk. In addition to the on-site Burnet Gallery, art is everywhere, including in each of the 60 guestrooms, because, as Rockwell says, "people don't want culture in prescribed pockets."

Special feature
The Chambers Kitchen. Jean-Georges Vongerichten oversees the restaurant, which gets rave reviews for its mouth-watering, Asian-influenced menu.

Can't miss
The bar. Take Prince's cue–Minneapolis's resident bad boy–to party like it's 1999 and head to the hotel's rooftop bar, Red, White and Fucking Blue. Named after a neon sign sculpture by Tracey Emin, the club is perfect for bringing the entourage (page 65, right). Angus Fairhurst's one-armed gorilla sculpture holds sway over the courtyard fire pit.

If there were lingering doubts of the Chamber's architectural and artistic edge, book a night in the Rock Star Suite (pages 62 to 63). The name says it all. From the art that decorates the walls to the floor-to-ceiling windows, from the insanely sexy white leather furnishings to the black hardwood floors, this is rock star chic at its most luxe. The parlor area opens to a wet bar, and is flanked by an enormous terrace. The bathroom, designed by Villeroy & Bloch, combines art, high design, and technology (page 65, left). It includes a rainfall shower; a deep soaking tub hidden behind a frosted glass window; and a large LCD TV-screen, which shows three-hours worth of avant-garde video art. And let's not forget the bed: Pillow-top mattress, black leather headboards, and 400-count sheets ensure a night of deep relaxation, something everyone craves, rock star or not.

Chambers
901 Hennepin Avenue
Minneapolis, Minnesota
T 612 767 6900
F 612 767 6801
www.chambersminneapolis.com

THERE ARE FAMOUS
WORKS OF ART
EVERYWHERE—HANGING
IN THE CORRIDORE, IN
THE BAR, AND IN EACH
OF THE 60 GUESTROOMS.

Location
**New York City,
United States**
Room
The Penthouse
Architect/Designer
Julian Schnabel
Rate
Expensive

ROOMS AT THE GRAMERCY ARE QUINTESSENTIAL NEW YORKERS: STYLISH, CLASSY, AND 100 PERCENT UNIQUE.

GRAMERCY PARK HOTEL

WITH AN EXTRAORDINARY
USE OF COLOR, THE ROOM
IS A SENSUOUS VISION OF
ARTFUL DIVERSITY.

THE ROSE BAR AND
JADE BAR ARE TWO
OF THE MOST ORIGINAL,
SOPHISTICATED, AND
EXCITING PUBLIC SPACES
IN NEW YORK CITY.

JULIAN SCHNABEL
PERSONALLY CHOSE
THE ANTIQUES AND
PHOTOGRAPHS FOR
THE TWO-BEDROOM
PENTHOUSE.

Gramercy Park Hotel was built in 1925 on the site of flamboyant architect Stanford White's home, previously the townhouse where Edith Wharton was born. Known as a meeting place for artists, adventurers, and bon vivants, the hotel hosted Humphrey Bogart's wedding, was home to humorist S. J. Perelman, and a second home to Babe Ruth, who liked to drink at the bar. When the chic, sleek atmosphere inevitably tarnished, this grande dame was given a makeover by no less than Ian Schrager—Mr. Big of the hotel industry.

With artist and filmmaker Julian Schnabel as designer, the recently renovated Gramercy Park Hotel takes on an idiosyncratic, eclectic, even whimsical personality. The lobby and public spaces feature a serious collection of antiques, custom-designed furniture by Schnabel, and contemporary art masterpieces by such artists as Jean-Michel Basquiat, Richard Prince, and, of course, Schnabel himself. Though this first-class gallery is fit for a museum, the space invites "lobby socializing," as do the Rose and Jade bars (pages 70 and 71).

The extraordinary two-bedroom Penthouse, like all 186 rooms, faces the exclusive, gated Gramercy Park (page 69 and page 72). The floorplan includes a living room, dining room, library, wood-paneled kitchen, a custom bathroom with a soaking tub and shower, and a multimedia center with a pair of oversized flat-screen TVs. Attention to detail is evident in the plastered lime walls created with a 600-year-old European technique, a mahogany wood ceiling, and an original Stanford White fireplace and mantel (pages 66 to 67). With carefully chosen antiques and a series of photographs curated by Schnabel, walking into this hotel is like entering a three-dimensional painting (page 68).

Schrager's genius—along with his late partner, Steve Rubell, he started Studio 54 and Palladium—lies in creating a buzz. He describes Gramercy Park Hotel as a place for the "new haute bohemian" who has "resources, taste, and understands the finer things in life." Wakiya, the hotel's restaurant, capitalizes on Schrager's star power and is backed by such powerhouses as Nobu Matsuhisa, Richie Notar, Meir Tepper, and Robert De Niro. The haute bohemian never had it so good.

Special feature
The spacious rooms. The hotel originally had 500 guestrooms. When Schrager reconfigured it to 185 rooms, he created some of the city's largest hotel quarters.

Can't miss
The Private Roof Club and Garden. With a retractable roof 16 stories above the city, this is one of New York City's most uniquely beautiful indoor/outdoor spaces.

Gramercy Park Hotel
2 Lexington Avenue
New York, NY 10010
T 212 920 3300
F 212 673 5890
www.gramercyparkhotel.com

Location
**New York City,
United States**
Room
Penthouse
Architect
Grzywinski Pons
Designer
Zaha Hadid
Rate
Expensive

AS ONE OF NEW YORK CITY'S NEWEST KIDS ON THE BLOCK, THE RIVINGTON IS HOME TO DESIGN-SAVVY GUESTS EAGER TO PARTAKE IN THE HIPSTER-HEAVY, NONSTOP ENERGY OF THE LOWER EAST SIDE.

HOTEL ON RIVINGTON

Although it was once an immigrant neighborhood, the Lower East Side is now the epicenter of cool—home to hipsters, students, and a host of galleries, bars, and boutiques. Its crowning achievement? The Hotel on Rivington. The building's 21 stories literally tower over the rest of the neighborhood, a sharp contrast to the area's low-rise brick tenement buildings. Rising from these humble surroundings, the hotel looks like a nightclub, complete with doormen who resemble bouncers.

There are 110 stunning guestrooms at the Rivington, but of all of these the Penthouse is a celebrity sight in its own right (pages 74 to 75 and 77). Lower East Side denizen Moby (whose tea shop and vegan café, Teany, is a block away) shot the cover photo of his album *Hotel* in there. Models Milla Jovovich and Carmen Hawk recently poised on-site for the cover of *Paper* magazine. But the triplex Penthouse is more than just an haute suite that hosts one glam photo shoot after another.

Special feature
Annie O. Named after its curator, Annie Ohayon, the hotel shop offers everything from Swissco toothbrushes to vintage Rolexes. Open until midnight, guests can shop with cocktail glass in hand.

Can't miss
Thor. Besides a diverse menu and kicking bar scene, the hotel's restaurant features a striking, 21-foot-high glass atrium dining room.

Although India Mahdavi decorated the hotel's elegant guestrooms, the Penthouse falls under the domain of Zaha Hadid, known for her sleek, bold use of space. The beige and brown furniture comes in an array of fabrics from suede to velvet to leather. Featuring a heated slate floor and a dark wood ceiling, the loftlike main floor is complete with a living room, a dining room that seats ten, and home theater. The mezzanine bedroom offers a separate fireplace alcove for lounging.

While the furnishings illustrate elegant restraint, Hahid lets the jaw-dropping 360-degree views of the New York skyline add the sizzle and pop. As the tallest building in the area, the Penthouse is a front-row ticket for one of the best views of the city. Since the cityscape takes center stage, the rest of the room's amenities—like the two-person Japanese soaking tub and the Jacuzzi that fits eight—are added bonuses. There's also an outdoor shower on the rooftop for those guests who want to release their inner exhibitionist.

The Hotel on Rivington is all about the views and the location. The lucky Penthouse guest can sample the flavor of the trendsetting neighborhood from any one of the hip restaurants—Schiller's anyone?—or simply by sitting on the rooftop, observing the humming nightlife.

Hotel on Rivington
107 Rivington Street
New York, NY 10002
T 212 475 2600
F 212 475 5959
www.hotelonrivington.com
info@hotelonrivington.com

A PREMIUM IS PLACED
ON THE FLOOR-TO-
CEILING GLASS WALLS,
GUARANTEEING THE
BEST VIEWS OF NEW
YORK CITY, PERIOD.

Location
Palm Springs,
United States
Room
Dorrington Villa
Architect/Designer
Kelly Wearstler
Rate
Expensive

STEPPING THROUGH THE
DOORS OF THE VICEROY IS
AKIN TO STEPPING INTO THE
DAYS OF OLD-TIME GLAMOUR
AND AUTHENTICITY.

VICEROY PALM SPRINGS

THE HOTEL BECAME
THE HIDEAWAY FOR
HOLLYWOOD'S GOLDEN-
ERA STARS, INCLUDING
CLARK GABLE AND
ERROL FLYNN.

Back in Hollywood's golden age, movie stars were contractually bound to stay within 100 miles of the studio when they were filming. When they wanted to escape, the drove to Palm Springs in the Coachella Valley, which happens to be 97 miles from the Hollywood sign. Framed by the San Jacinto mountain peaks, this valley, filled with sage, mesquite, and Joshua trees, made a perfect hideaway and playground for the glamorous and famous. Palm Springs gained notoriety in the 1950s and 1960s thanks to the Rat Pack–Frank Sinatra, Dean Martin, Sammy Davis, Jr., Peter Lawford, and Joey Bishop–who used to enjoy steak and martini dinners at nearby Melvyn's Restaurant and Lounge. Prior to their heyday, the hotel had seen the likes of Joan Crawford, Errol Flynn, and Clark Gable.

The Viceroy has retained its golden-era style with a decidedly contemporary twist that designer Kelly Wearstler describes as "modern glamor." Her challenge at the Viceroy was to restore luster and dignity. In the lobby, vibrant yellow walls suggest the warmth of Palm Springs, while crisp white furnishings echo the desert's sand-swept environment. The 68 low-lying guestrooms (built as bungalows in the 1930s) sprawl over four landscaped acres and include studios, suites, and private villas.

Arranged around three separate pool areas, the design strategy blends interior and exterior space.

With its garden-level access, the Dorrington Villa is the one to go for. The chic black-and-white scheme is brightened with vivid pops of citrus color, like a lemon armchair or a brilliant yellow lamp (pages 78 to 79). Equipped with multiple fireplaces, a kitchen, and plenty of lounge areas and patio space (page 80, right), it's no wonder celebs sought out the hotel as a refuge among friends. Quaintly private yet uniquely accessible, the villa is located between the two adults-only pool positioned among the lush garden (page 80, left). Finishing touches include complimentary totes and shoes, trays full of healthy drinks, and all-weekend gourmet barbeques–poolside, of course. In high summer, one of the Jacuzzis® is chilled to create an ice-plunge for pure refreshment.

So many features of the Viceroy suggest the somewhat campy allure and sybaritic charms of old Hollywood glitz, but the luxurious accommodations and amenities exert an appeal of their own for the Beverly Hills party set. At the Viceroy, guests can choose a quiet, secluded getaway weekend or a scene that is undeniably close to the action. Or, perhaps, a bit of both.

Special feature
The Estrella spa and fitness center. This center boasts a yoga terrace, couples' massage suite, and outdoor massage cabanas, along with dozens of options for great pampering.

Can't miss
The Citron Restaurant. Graphic white wallpaper is used not only on the walls but also on the ceiling. Lunch offers an array of soups, salads, sandwiches, and tapas; dinner is an elegant experience showcasing California cuisine with such treats as saffron seafood risotto with mussels. The mostly California wine list is particularly memorable.

Viceroy Palm Springs
415 South Belardo Road
Palm Springs, CA 92262
T 760 320 4117
F 760 323 3303
www.viceroypalmsprings.com
viceroyps-concierge@thekorgroup.com

ASIA/F

PACIFIC

Location
**Falls Creek,
Australia**
Room
Penthouse
Architect/Designer
Elenberg Fraser
Rate
Expensive

**HOME TO AUSTRALIA'S
KILLER SLOPES, THIS
SKI RESORT IS WITHOUT
PEER—WINTER OR SUMMER.**

HUSKI

THE DESIGN WAS
INSPIRED BY THE
RANDOM ANGLES
OF SNOWFLAKE
SEGMENTS.

GUESTS CAN SKI RIGHT
OUT ONTO THE SLOPES
FROM THE PENTHOUSE,
OR ENJOY A SOAK IN THE
TUB ON THE BALCONY.

Surrounded by panoramic views of the Australian Alps, the Huski hotel is a paradise for winter sports from June to September because of the pristine powdery snow and groomed slopes. In the summer months, from December to March, the hillsides are filled with wildflowers.

Eschewing the traditional alpine lodge look, Huski follows a radial design modeled on the segments of a snowflake (pages 84 to 87). The 14 self-contained apartments range from a studio to a penthouse. The lodge received *Alpine Style*'s Best Exterior and Best Food awards in its first year, and continues to win kudos from the opposite side of the globe with *Wallpaper* magazine's 2006 design award for architecture. But the stylish exterior is only part of the story.

This lodge is all about attentive, one-on-one service. Upon entering, guests are welcomed from the kitchen of the Huski produce store rather than signing in at a reception desk. The store offers gourmet snacks and a wine bar.

Inside the room of choice, the split-level Penthouse, stark white walls and clean surfaces dominate a comfortable floorplan of four bedrooms, four baths, a living area, and an open kitchen (page 88). A spacious private balcony with hot tub overlooks the valley, mountains, and the town of Falls Creek. The elegant but comfortable furniture is custom designed, and every room features charming decorative details, such as cowhides and hand-knitted throws. The penthouse sleeps up to ten people, making it the ideal get-away for a group ski trip. The deluxe amenities include in-floor slab heating, ski-in/ski-out access, and lift access from each floor.

At Huski, the friendly staff and their attention to detail has redefined the concept of service in alpine resorts.

Special feature
The spa. After a vigorous day of power-skiing or hiking, the Endota Spa provides signature treatments, including a herb and oil scrub, clay body wrap, and massage. The communal hot tub offers the perfect relaxation amid snow-capped peaks.

Can't miss
World-class skiing. Falls Creek has something for everyone—from expert slopes to one of the longest beginner slopes in the world.

Huski
3 Sitzmark Street
Falls Creek, Victoria, Australia
T 61 1300 65 22 60
www.huski.com.au
bookings@huski.com.au

Location
**Tasmania,
Australia**
Architect/Designer
Ken Latona
Rate
Expensive

THE INTREPID TREKKER
WHO TAKES ON BAY OF
FIRES GETS A WILDERNESS
ADVENTURE AND A FIVE-STAR
HOTEL EXPERIENCE.

BAY OF FIRES LODGE

THE GUEST LIST
READS LIKE AN ECLECTIC
MIX OF WHO'S WHO
AND INCLUDES TYCOONS,
HOLLYWOOD STARS,
AND OTHER VIPS.

For the ultimate Robinson Crusoe-like experience, Tasmania's Bay of Fires can't be beat. With hundreds of miles of steep cliffs, glacial valleys, and rain forests, Tasmania offers a diversity of habitats, including modern hotels, restaurants, and boutiques in Hobart, the capital. Shirking the city, Bay of Fires has made its home deep in the woods of Mount William National Park. In order to stay at the lodge, guests must participate in a four-day walk that takes them around the national park: White sandy beaches, granite outcrops, and a sweeping coastline (page 95).

The first night of the walk is spent in the fully appointed Forester beach camp–a structure built of wooden flooring positioned a few feet from the beach (pages 90 to 91). The second day is spent exploring and walking to the Bay of Fires lodge (pages 92 to 93). The lodge is the architectural high point of the four-day stay, though by no means does it distract from the surrounding natural beauty. Most of the lodge's materials were flown in from Hobart by helicopter (so as not to leave vehicular footprints), and the remaining ones were carried in by hand. Sustainable resources like hardwood and plantation pine were used. Energy efficiency is a must. Roof water is collected and stored for use in the bathrooms and kitchens. A solar panel provides power for all lighting, composting toilet ventilation, and fan-driven gas convection heaters.

Tasmania has largely survived as one of the world's last wild places because of its geography, climate, and a tourist trade that values the environment. Preservation is a matter of redemption here and once guests arrive at Bay of Fires, it's easy to understand why. With land this beautiful, it's worth the trek to go green.

Special feature
The food. With complimentary wine included in the chef-prepared meals, this camp cuisine can rival any five-star restaurant.

Can't miss
The Eastern Grey kangaroo. The Mount William National Park was established to preserve the world's last remaining habitat for this kangaroo.

Bay of Fires Lodge
P.O. Box 1879
Launceston 7250
Tasmania, Australia
www.bayoffires.com.au

WITH CHEF-PREPARED
MEALS, COMPLIMENTARY
WINE, AND A BEAUTIFUL
BEACH, GOING GREEN
IS EASY.

Location
**Hong Kong,
China**
Room
**L600 Landmark
Spa Corner Room**
Architect
**Aedas Limited and
Kohn Pedersen Fox**
Designer
Peter Remedios
Rate
Expensive

WITH ONE OF ASIA'S
BEST SPAS ON-SITE,
THE LANDMARK
IS HONG KONG'S
CROWNING JEWEL.

LANDMARK
MANDARIN
ORIENTAL

Extra space for kicking back is a much coveted and pricey commodity in Hong Kong. The Landmark Mandarin Oriental, however, eschews the mandate for spatial efficiency in its guestrooms, all 113 of which are designed with a sense of ample-sized proportions by esteemed hotel-interior wizard Peter Remedios (who hails from decidedly roomier Los Angeles). His hallmark creation, the L600 Landmark Spa Corner Room, is the largest guestroom in Hong Kong, and cocoons guests in tranquility in the face of the frenetic energy of the city's haute central district (pages 96 to 97).

Remedios's design synthesizes the traditional comforts of home with a flair for the supremely modern. The truth is in the details—there's an interplay of rich and dark African wenge wood with sleek silver inlay and an abundance of glass. The tone is decidedly masculine, and the simple furniture contributes to the unadorned lines. The orchids brought in daily complement the room's color scheme—deep ebonies and zebranos offset by soft whites and creamy beiges. Remedios succeeded in combining the cosmopolitanism of the city with its status as undeniably non-Western.

Special feature
The door-to-door service. The moment guests deplane, the hotel's airport concierge escorts them through immigration, baggage collection, and customs, and arranges the transportation.

Can't miss
The Sanctuary Suite. This v700-square-foot private room inside the Oriental Spa can be privately rented. Equipped with an amethyst crystal steam-shower, vitality tub, dual massage beds, personal vanity and changing area, and flat-screen TV, it's a personal haven that can be enjoyed for three hours at a

The nucleus of the L600 is the bathroom, which, girded in glass, is not for the room-sharer bent on absolute privacy (page 99, right). The 7-foot spherical bathtub mirrors in miniature the 200-square-foot imprint of the room itself. In the spirit of cocooning, the room has spa amenities. The shower gels, soaps, and massage oils are subtlety infused with ylang-ylang and lavender to ensure sensual soothing, while a soak in the rainfall shower is supplemented by a state-of-the-art entertainment system, including a high-definition flat-screen TV, one of three in the L600. For those who prefer to avoid the traffic-choked streets of the city but still wish to remain connected, the Landmark doesn't skimp on gadgetry. Digital phone displays provide guest names, and a technology butler descends upon the room at the slightest hint of a problem or question.

Amber, the hotel's restaurant, and the award-winning Oriental Spa, lauded by some as the best in Asia, maintain a guest's serenity. Those who venture beyond the Landmark's doors will immediately encounter a ton of designer boutiques—Gucci, Chanel, and Celine among them. A sanctuary amid Hong Kong's bustling streets, the hotel is a landmark itself.

Landmark Mandarin Oriental, Hong Kong
15 Queen's Road Central
Hong Kong, China
T 852 2132 0188
F 852 2132 0199
www.mandarinoriental.com/landmark/
lmhkg-enquiry@mohg.com

ORCHIDS ARE BROUGHT
IN DAILY TO ADD ANOTHER
TOUCH OF SERENITY
(AND LUXURY).

Location
**Jaipur,
India**
Room
Kohinoor Villa
Architect
**Prabhat Patki
and Associates**
Designer
**H. L. Lim
and Associates**
Rate
Expensive

FROM ITS PRINCELY TENTS
TO ITS OPULENT VILLAS, THE
PALATIAL OBEROI RAJVILAS
IS A TRUE SHOW-STOPPER.

THE OBEROI
RAJVILAS

THIRTY-TWO ACRES OF
LOTUS-FILLED PONDS
AND BLOOMING GARDENS,
PRIVATE COURTYARDS
AND REFLECTION POOLS
COULD EXPLAIN WHY THE
HOTEL IS A MAINSTAY
FOR SUCH HIGH-PROFILE
GUESTS AS BILL CLINTON.

VILLA GUESTS CAN
RELAX INSIDE THE
WALLED GARDEN
OR IN THE PRIVACY
OF THEIR OWN POOL
AND SAUNA.

The Oberoi Rajvilas is a maharajah's fantasy of lotus-filled ponds, blooming gardens, and lavish architecture, located on 32 acres of exotic Indian landscape (pages 100 to 101). Pavilions and reflection pools dot the hotel's property, providing a picture-perfect backdrop that would satisfy any prince. With 54 guestrooms, 14 luxury tents, 1 villa, and the deluxe Kohinoor Villa, this hotel is akin to a small village. Every space is clustered around private courtyards in a manner befitting a royal fort, which may explain why it's a mainstay with high-profile personalities like Bill Clinton. Even the owner chose the hotel as the place to celebrate his daughter's extravagant wedding.

Of course, every prince must have his king and in this case, the daddy of them all is the Kohinoor Villa, reachable by crossing a small moat bridge (page 102, left). Featuring a regal teak four-poster bed and sunken white marble bathtub that overlooks its own private walled ornamental garden, this villa has two bedrooms and a private dining room as well as a private swimming pool. The master suite also includes an en suite sauna. The furniture is a testament to the quality of fine Indian craftsmanship and works in tandem with the area's rich artistic history. Bright colors, sumptuous materials, and superb service are de rigeur here, raising the bar for every other hotel looking for the five-star stamp.

The Kohinoor diamond was once the largest known diamond in the world and the object of countless feuds, victories, romances, and mystery. It's no surprise that the Kohinoor Villa at Oberoi Rajvilas is the hotelier's gem of India.

Special feature
The swimming pool. Flanked by two sandstone torches and two exquisitely domed chattris, this 60-foot-long pool is but one of the hotel's special features. A croquet area, golf course, and jogging track round out the hotel's stellar amenities.

Can't miss
The elephant safari. For a traditional trek through the Indian countryside, guests can go on an elephant safari, some 20 minutes away from the hotel. Afterward there's a picnic at the base of Nailia Fort.

The Oberoi Rajvilas
Goner Road
Jaipur, Rajasthan 303 012, India
T 91 141 268 0101
F 91 141 268 0202
www.oberoi-rajvilas.com
gm@oberoi-rajvilas.com

Location
**Rajasthan,
India**
Room
Devi Garh Suite
Architect
Navin Gupta
Designer
Rajiv Saini
Rate
Expensive

PERCHED ATOP A GIANT CLIFF, THE LAVISH DEVI GARH IS THAT MUCH CLOSER TO THE HEAVENS—AND SO ARE THE GUESTS WHO STAY HERE.

DEVI GARH

A TOUR OF THE NEARBY
HILLS BY CAMEL IS A
SPECIAL FEATURE OF THIS
RENOVATED EIGHTEENTH-
CENTURY PALACE.

THIS IS TRULY A UNIQUE
PLACE WHERE THE PAST
MEETS THE FUTURE.

The Devi Garh is nestled in the age-old Aravali hills of Rajasthan (page 113, bottom). The actual construction of the structure began in the 1760s, but was abandoned in the 1960s. Today, the Devi Garh has regained its place of privilege, after much restoration and reconstruction. The 39 suites are designed in a compelling mix of the palatial and contemporary, accented by local marble and colorful tiles.

Special feature
The on-site astrologer. Contemplating being social but would prefer tucking in for a romantic night? Consult the Devi astrologer to set things right.

Can't miss
Camel rides. Embark on a tour planned by the reception desk of the Aravali hills in old-school style—via camel back.

The hotel's premium suite, the Devi Garh Suite, is literally a treasure. Its white marble interiors are offset by the vibrant inlays of semiprecious stones—malachite, mother of pearl, jasper, and lapis lazuli. The suite has a black marble swimming pool (pages 106 to 107, and page 111), sun deck, and Jacuzzi® (page 110). Huge windows overlook the Aravali hills and the courtyard with a modern fountain and swing. It is available on its own or in combination with the Aravali Suite (page 108 and page 109, bottom right). The combination of these two suites mingles the male and female energies of Shiv—the Hindu god of destruction—and Shakti—his divine consort.

Devi Garh
Devigarh, Delwara NH-8, Nathdwara
District Rajasmand,
Rajasthan 313 202, India
T 91 2953 289 211
F 91 2953 289 357
www.deviresorts.com
devigarh@deviresorts.com

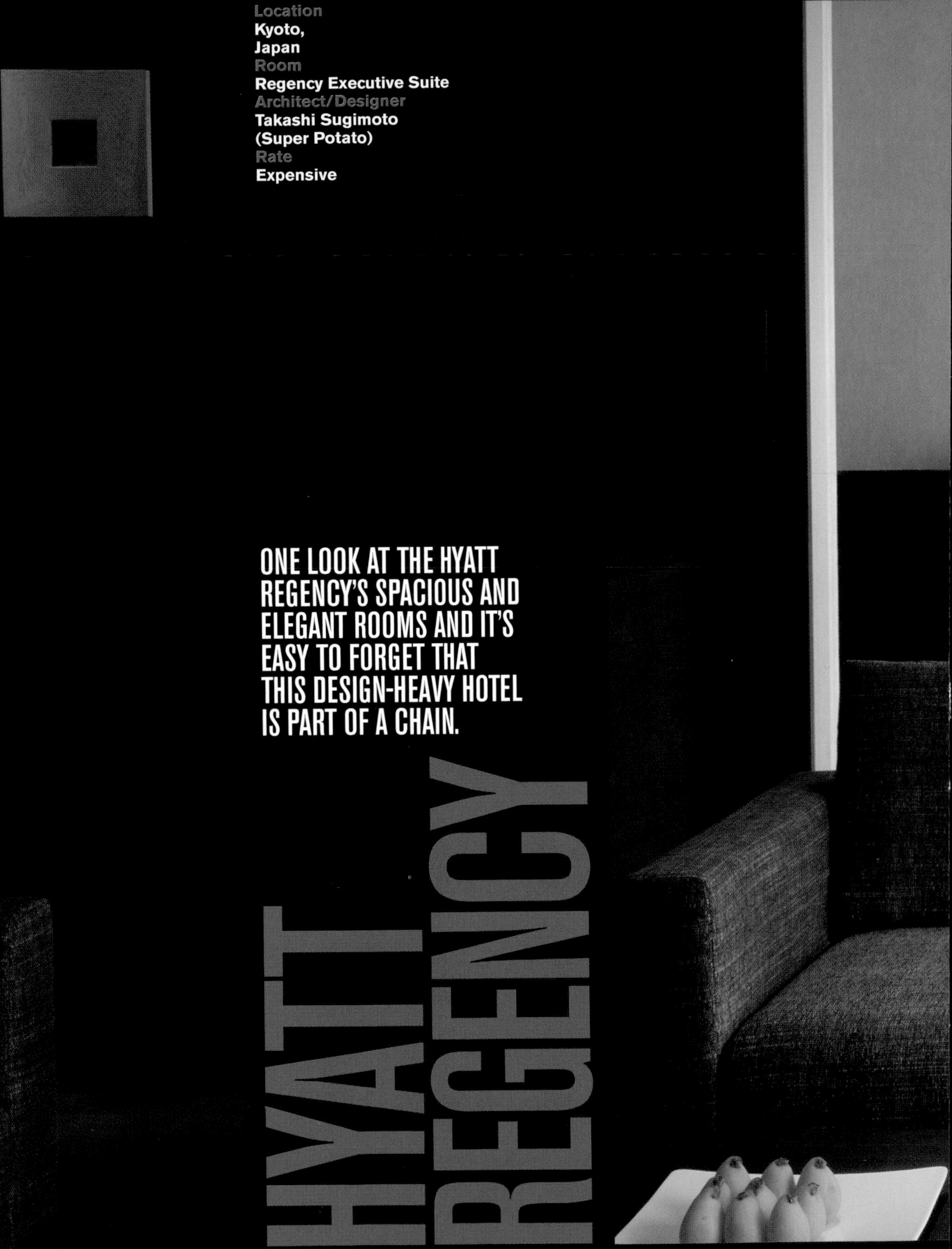

Location
**Kyoto,
Japan**
Room
Regency Executive Suite
Architect/Designer
**Takashi Sugimoto
(Super Potato)**
Rate
Expensive

ONE LOOK AT THE HYATT
REGENCY'S SPACIOUS AND
ELEGANT ROOMS AND IT'S
EASY TO FORGET THAT
THIS DESIGN-HEAVY HOTEL
IS PART OF A CHAIN.

HYATT
REGENCY

GUESTS CAN
CONSULT THE ON-SITE
ACUPUNCTURIST AND
GET INDIVIDUALIZED
TREATMENTS DURING
THEIR STAY.

Located in the secluded area of Higashiyama Shichijo in Kyoto, the Hyatt Regency is a 189-room hotel on seven floors.

The hotel's renovation was overseen by Takashi Sugimoto, the owner and principal designer at Tokyo's Super Potato. Known for creating nontraditional hotel interiors, Super Potato combines earthy Japanese traditionalism and international contemporary design to give the Hyatt Regency Kyoto its intimate ambiance. The smartly elegant Regency Executive Suite offers the best mix of Japanese and Western countries, featuring natural walnut walls and rich fabrics to create a residential ambiance (pages 114 to 115 and page 116, left). The wooden bathroom comes complete with a separate deep-soaking bathtub and wet area, while the Japanese tatami living room is outfitted with a sunken *kotatsu* table (page 116, right). Large windows overlook a traditional Japanese garden decorated with a waterfall and pond. The overall effect is stunning yet simple, making the suite feel high-end and comfortable at the same time.

Excellent dining is available at the Italian-style trattoria, the Grill, with an open kitchen and wood-burning ovens, and a Japanese restaurant featuring *kappo*-style cuisine with a charcoal grill counter and a sushi and *touzan* bar.

Special feature
The Ishoku Dogen package. Guests are consulted about their health by an on-site acupuncturist and receive three acupuncture sessions during a two-night stay. After each treatment, they enjoy a special tea made from over 20 kinds of grain. The dinner menu is tailored to each guest's health conditions.

Can't miss
Several temples and museums are within walking distance of the hotel. The rectangular hall of the Sanjusangendo Temple, dating from 1164, is filled with 1,001 carved and gilded statues of a standing Kannon (the Bodhisattya of Mercy).

Hyatt Regency Kyoto
644-2 Sanjusangendo-mawari
Higashiyama-ku, Kyoto
605-0941, Japan
T 81 75 541 1234
F 81 75 541 2203
www.kyoto.regency.hyatt.com
info@hyattregencykyoto.com

Location
**Fesdu Island,
Maldives**
Room
Ocean Haven
Architect/Designer
**ECO-ID Architects
and Poole Associates**
Rate
Expensive

THE W HOTEL EXPERIENCE
FINDS NEW LIFE IN THE
MALDIVES, A SANCTUARY SO
EXTRAORDINARY IT BORDERS
ON TRANSCENDENCE.

W RETREAT AND SPA

Ideal for anyone who favors white sand beaches and pristine waters, the W Retreat and Spa in Maldives is more than a resort; it is a lifestyle destination for those in search of tropical extravagance. The star-studded W experience begins even in transit: Once guests deplane from the Male airport, they receive an attaché filled with travel-friendly accoutrements for the 25-minute seaplane ride to the private island. On the ground, a fleet of staff members whisk guests, via individual golf buggies, to the main reception area.

The 78 villas feature vast expanses of curving decks, comfortable chaise lounges, and gorgeous driftwood furniture. Open to warm sea breezes and panoramic views of the Indian Ocean, these villas ingeniously combine traditional Maldivian elements and indigenous materials with more modern amenities. While every villa is a gem, the Ocean Haven is the most deserving of praise. Here, glass-paneled flooring offers glimpses of the colorful sea life below (page 121, top). At night, underwater lights illuminate the flora, starfish, and other sea life to brilliant effect. Floor-to-ceiling glass walls slide open, allowing the outside in and vice versa. The wraparound deck extends the living quarters, offering several areas for both private respite and social entertaining (page 118 to 119). This merging of inside and out imbues an open, flexible quality, encouraging guests to interact with the surrounding natural beauty.

The villa's décor is ultrachic and lives up to the W's signature style. Inspired by the island's natural colors and textures, cream-colored fabrics and throw pillows complement dark, unobtrusive wood detailing (page 121, bottom). The furniture itself is roomy—the plush W king-sized bed is the focal point of the bedroom, and large circular daybeds dot the lounge and pool areas. An oversized bathtub and cathedral ceiling round out the master bedroom, while the junior suite has a twin bed and private bathroom. Equipped with a lagoon, big plasma TVs, and an oversized plunge pool with Jacuzzi® seats, the Ocean Haven elevates the hotel experience to a new level.

Special Feature

The Whatever/Whenever service. Ever wanted a birthday party at 35,000 feet? Or a private scuba lessons from a leading marine biologist? A bathtub of chocolate? The Whatever/Wherever Service staff transform your wildest dreams into fantasy—just so long as it's legal, that is.

Can't miss

Fire. The gourmand delights of this barbeque are served in a rustic, outdoor environment. The casual fare is a perfect accompaniment to the live acoustic music and local *boduberu* dance performance.

W Retreat and Spa – Maldives
Fesdu Island, North Ari Atoll, Maldives
T 960 666 2222
F 960 666 2200
www.whotels.com/maldives
wmaldives.welcome@whotels.com

THE GLASS-PANELED
FLOORS GIVE GLIMPSES
OF THE COLORFUL
SEA LIFE BELOW.

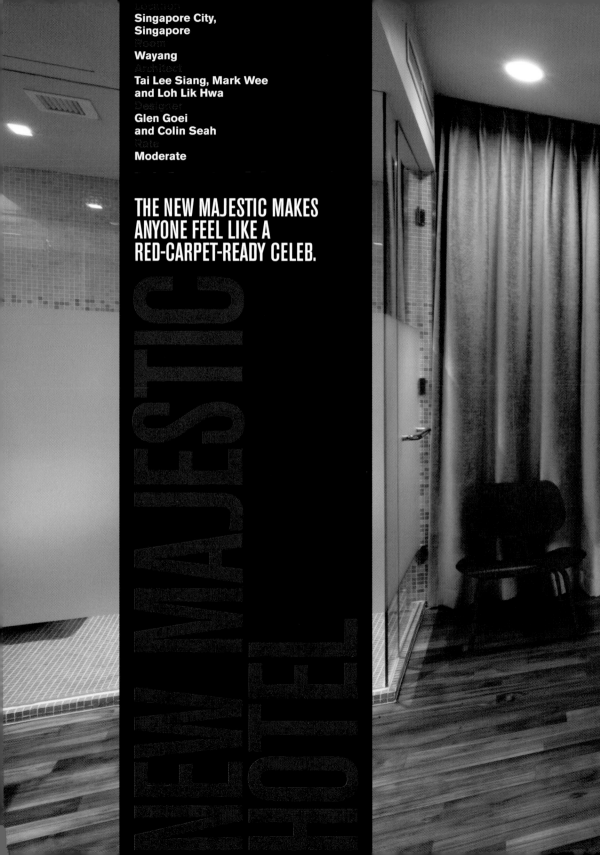

Location
**Singapore City,
Singapore**
Room
Wayang
Architect
**Tai Lee Siang, Mark Wee
and Loh Lik Hwa**
Designer
**Glen Goei
and Colin Seah**
Rate
Moderate

THE NEW MAJESTIC MAKES ANYONE FEEL LIKE A RED-CARPET-READY CELEB.

NEW MAJESTIC HOTEL

PERFECT FOR THOSE
WHO LIKE TO WATCH
AND BE WATCHED.

THE FILMS OF ZHANG
YIMOU INSPIRED THE
ROOM'S DECOR: SILK
WALLS AND CUSTOMIZED
CALLIGRAPHY PANELS.

Lawyer-turned-hotel-owner Loh Lik Peng, who remembered dining in the original Majestic Hotel, has revamped the art deco building to its former glory while instilling a refreshing modern approach (pages 124, page 125, and page 127). Located on a historical street better known for housing wealthy men's mistresses, the New Majestic coyly plays with Chinese traditionalism and highlights some of the original hotel's best features. The lobby ceiling, for example, has been stripped back unevenly to reveal the layers of paint that have covered it over the years.

The hotel's 30 rooms revolve around one of four thematic principles: Mirror rooms, perfect for those who like to watch and be watched, have mirrors that stretch across the walls and ceiling. Hanging Bed rooms have murals that cover whole walls; Loft rooms have beds that rest on slender columns so that the sleeping chamber floats in a light-filled attic space (pages 122 to 123, and page 126); and Aquarium rooms feature a glass-enclosed central bathtub with views of the sleeping space and balcony. Separate from these four thematically organized rooms are five concept rooms. The one to book is called Wayang (page 126).

Designer Glen Goei, a critically acclaimed film and theater director, was inspired by the films of Zhang Yimou (*Raise the Red Lantern* and *House of Flying Daggers*) to create this almost all-red room. Goei outfitted the room with sumptuous silk walls, Chinese lanterns, and customized calligraphy panels. The rich fabrics evoke the nostalgia of Imperial China's performing troupes. Like the other rooms, the floors are made of Burmese teak.

Further enhancing the room's majestic experience is the hotel's Cantonese-inspired restaurant, which has 2,000 bottles in its wine cellar. With artwork from up and coming Chinese artists scattered throughout the hotel's public spaces, the New Majestic Hotel expertly fuses together local culture, stylish design, and artistic vision.

Special feature
The sculptural centerpiece in the restaurant. This modern brass-and-copper sculpture is from the *Ode to Homeland* series by Cai Zhi Song, one of China's most prestigious sculptors. It's another piece in the Majestic's already impressive art collection.

Can't miss
The swimming pool (page 128). With portholes cut into the ceiling of the Majestic Restaurant, swimmers literally cross over the holes and their reflections cast shadows onto the diners' tables below. Voyeurism has never been so delicious.

New Majestic Hotel
31-37 Bukit Pasoh Road
Singapore 089845
T 65 6511 4700
www.newmajestichotel.com
reservations@newmajestichotel.com

Location
**Tangalle,
Sri Lanka**
Room
Ocean Suite
Architect/Designer
Kerry Hill
Rate
Expensive

THIS RESORT PULLS OUT
ALL THE STOPS TO MAINTAIN
ITS REP AS THE GO-TO
PLACE FOR A WORLD-CLASS
ROMANTIC HIDEAWAY.

AMANWELLA

THE RESORT'S NAME
COMES FROM THE
WORDS FOR "PEACE"
AND "BEACH."

Amanwella delights with its golden sand beach in a crescent-shaped cove, fringed with palm and coconut trees. The name of the resort derives from *aman*, or peace in Sanskrit, and *wella*, the Sinhalese word for beach. The peaceful ambiance begins as one enters the pebbled courtyard from the village road and passes through an open, tranquil water garden and open-air pavilion (page 135, bottom). Two grassy courtyards are separated by an excellent library that has a wide selection of books, including rare, out-of-print editions (page 135, top).

All of the hotel's 30 suites, linked by pathways through the coconut grove, are identical in their layout and design and fall into two categories based on their location and views of either the coconut grove or the ocean. In the ocean suites, architect Kerry Hill combined local materials and styles, such as the distinctive terracotta roof tiles and hand-hewn stone walls. The result is a design that is simultaneously rugged and sophisticated. Floor-to-ceiling lattice and glass panels form two sides of the suite's interior (page 137). These sliding-door panels open onto a private, walled-in courtyard on one side and on the other to a terrace (page 134, left). Inside, wooden sliding doors reveal a king-sized bed, writing desk, armchair with footstool, and credenza with personal bar. Guests can configure these sliding door panels in any way to create a wide-open room. Whether relaxing on the terrace or in the bath (pages 132 to 133), guests can appreciate a full view of the resort's natural beauty.

During the winter months, guests at the hotel can enjoy swimming and snorkeling (complimentary equipment available); in summer, the cooling onshore breeze creates ideal conditions for strolls and sunbathing. Year-round bathing is also available in Amanwella's central pool, as well as the private plunge pools in each of the suites.

But the main reason to vacation at Amanwella is the promise of serenity—an escape from the stress and noise of everyday life on one of the quietest beaches on the island. Guests lucky enough to enjoy the Aman experience are assured a kind of poetry of space unlike anywhere else in the world.

Special feature
The Beach Club. Located in the coconut grove just a few feet from the sea, this open pavilion is ideal for lounging and informal dining.

Can't miss
Nature walks. The salt pans at Bundala National Park attract a vast number of migratory shore birds (around 150 reported species). Uda Walawe National Park is best known for large herds of elephants, spotted deer, langur monkeys, and water buffalo.

Amanwella
Bodhi Mawatha
Wella Wathuara
Godellawela, Tangalle, Sri Lanka
T 94 47 224 1333
F 94 47 224 1334
www.amanresorts.com
amanwella@amanresorts.com

GUESTS CAN CONFIGURE
THE SLIDING DOORS TO CREATE
A WIDE-OPEN SPACE—THE
BETTER TO APPRECIATE THE
SURROUNDING ENVIRONMENT.

EUR

OPE

Location
**Graz,
Austria**
Room
Double Room
Architect
Günther Domenig
Designer
Andreas Thaler
Rate
Expensive

ROOMS AT THE AUGARTEN
INSTILL GUESTS WITH THE
DISTINCT FEELING THAT
ART AND ARCHITECTURE
ARE VERY MUCH ALIVE
AND WELL IN AUSTRIA.

AUGARTEN
HOTEL

THE HOTEL HAS BECOME
A SHOWCASE FOR OVER
250 ARTISTS TO DISPLAY
THEIR WORK.

The old town of Graz happens to be one of the largest historically intact architectural cities of the German-speaking world. This is not to say Graz is mired in the past. The opposite, in fact: This area flourishes with new ideas, and the 56-guestroom Augartenhotel stands as a prime example.

While the glass-and metal-framed exterior of the Augarten is a stark statement of modernity, its interior is pleasantly warm, with chestnut-hued wood floors and colorful art work (page 142). The hotel has quickly become a city landmark and a showcase for over 250 artists. The entire design of the hotel is imbued with a kind of intellectual playfulness—a prime example of such sophisticated whimsy is evident in the juxtaposition of a twenty-first century, red aluminum Rosso desk by Austrian designer Andreas Thaler paired with Verner Panton's 1960s cantilevered plastic chair. Every space is used as a creative opportunity, such as the indoor pool surrounded by rainbow-colored Supra sofas, designed by Thaler. In the lobby, furniture by Cappellini and Ligne Roset further encourages the eclecticism that bonds design and art–in this case, tons of it. Art is everywhere, graciously displayed atop surfaces, on the walls, and throughout each of the guestrooms designed by Günther Domenig. Stimulation isn't solely provided by the artistic surroundings, however. There is a sauna, solarium, rooftop terrace, and the award-winning restaurant Magnolia, which serves light fish dishes and just-picked veggies.

Special feature
The 24-hour bar. Need we say more?

Can't miss
The architecture. In the last few years, groundbreaking public buildings have been erected in the city. The most famous of these include the Kunsthaus and the Murinsel, an island made of steel situated in the river, containing a café, an open-air theater, and a playground.

No other guestroom synthesizes art and a sense of well being better than the Augarten's spacious Double Large Room (pages 140 to 141). Here, Domenig's reputation as the "architect of the game" is apparent. Guests are invited to "play" in the sitting area with straightforward, streamlined furnishings, on the plush king-sized bed, or in the ample-sized bathtub. A restrained gray-and-white color scheme dominates the room, enlivened with accents of vermilion and black. The balcony overlooks the hotel's courtyard. If working is absolutely necessary, a desk and workstation are provided.

Though Graz harmoniously blends architecture, artistic movements, and cultural styles dating back to the Middle Ages, its independent character is distinctly its own. To soak in the whole city, visit the hotel's rooftop terrace where Gustav Troger's elongated sculpture *Jochen Rindt* contemplates the view in kind.

Augartenhotel
Schönaugasse 53
8010 Graz, Austria
T 43 (0) 316 20 800
F 43 (0) 316 20 800/80
www.augartenhotel.at
office@augartenhotel.at

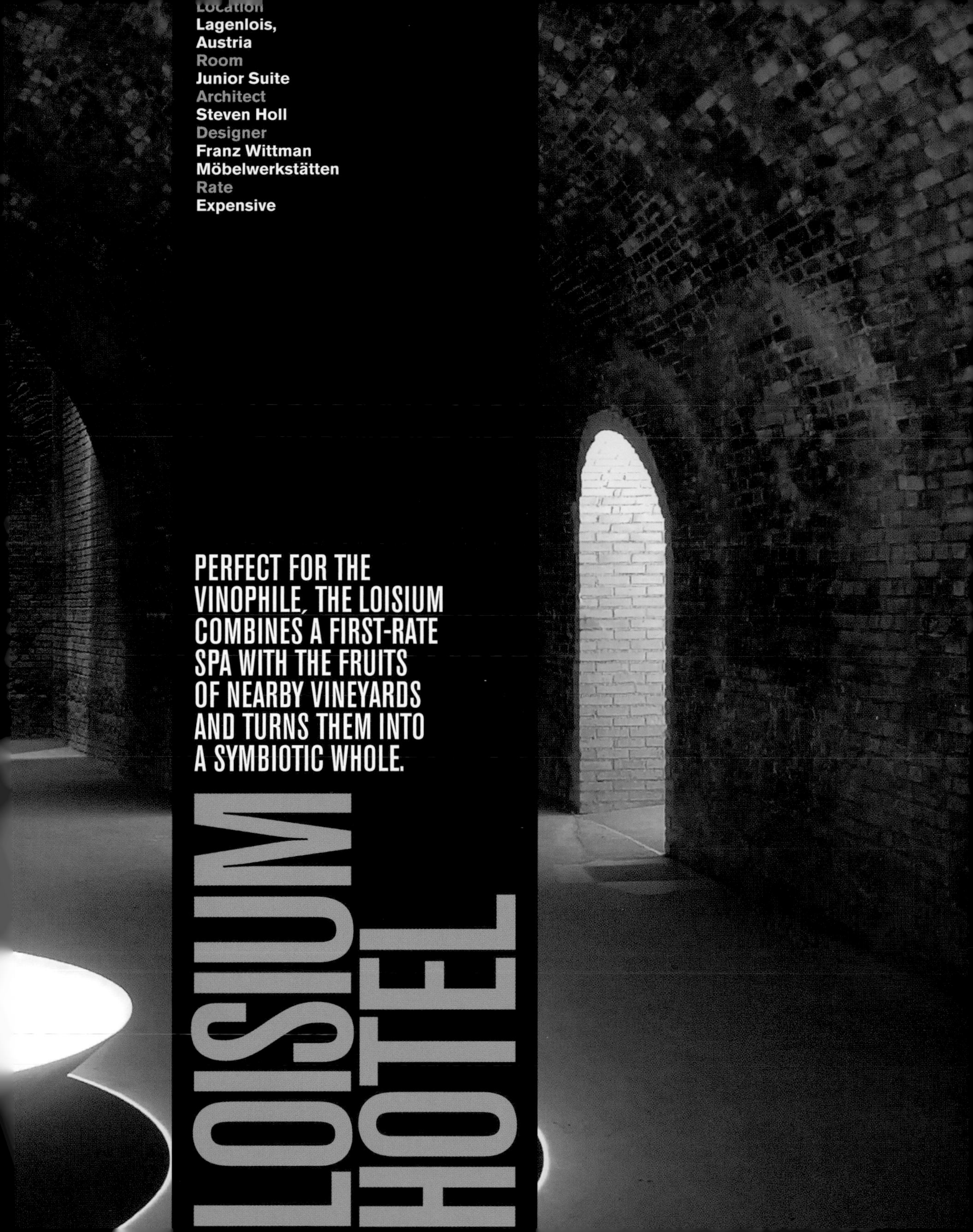

Location
**Lagenlois,
Austria**
Room
Junior Suite
Architect
Steven Holl
Designer
**Franz Wittman
Möbelwerkstätten**
Rate
Expensive

PERFECT FOR THE
VINOPHILE, THE LOISIUM
COMBINES A FIRST-RATE
SPA WITH THE FRUITS
OF NEARBY VINEYARDS
AND TURNS THEM INTO
A SYMBIOTIC WHOLE.

LOISIUM
HOTEL

THE LOISIUM'S LOBBY FLOOR IS MADE OF GLASS, GIVING THE ILLUSION THAT THE REST OF THE HOTEL IS FLOATING MID-AIR.

A spa for vinophiles—what could be better? The Langenlois region of Austria has fast been on the rise as the wonder of the wine world, and surrounded by lush vineyards, guests are aware that the Loisium Hotel is serious about this reputation. The hotel was designed by noted New York architect Steven Holl who wanted to created a kind of "floating" hotel that glows incandescent at night (page 149, bottom). The lobby floor is primarily made of glass and below it there is a pool, giving the appearance (and some may say sensation) that the Loisium gracefully hovers above ground (page 147). Or that could be the wine talking. The hotel sits above intricate vaults that resemble a labyrinthian maze of hooks and crannies (pages 144 to 145).

Of the hotel's 82 rooms, the Junior Suite is the most ample in size and offers a serene view of the rolling landscape. The room's architectural details and interior design elements serve as constant reminders of the relationship between vintner and hotelier.

Special feature
Vinotherapy. One of the hotel's many specialties is its series of spa treatments that incorporate grape and wine products.

Can't miss
The lobby furniture, which was created for Peggy Guggenheim in 1942 (page 149, right). Replicas are available.

Lamp bases are made of cork, glass latticework reminiscent of vines abounds, and the map of the 900-year-old underground vault and cellar appears as a pattern on the bed's comforter and on the living room sofa (page 149, right). There's nothing splashy about the suite—it has clean white walls, dark wood, lots of light, and custom-made furniture by the Wittman Carpentry Workshop. The open bathroom offers vineyard views (page 146, left and 149, top). Here, it's all about the wine. What more could anyone need, except a reason to relax.

Loisium Hotel
Loisium Allee 2
3550 Langenlois, Austria
T 43 (0) 2734 77 100
www.loisiumhotel.at
hotel@loisium.at

EVEN THE LIVING ROOM SOFA IS
DECORATED WITH A MAP OF A
900-YEAR-OLD WINE CELLAR
—A REMINDER THAT THE HOTEL
TAKES WINE SERIOUSLY.

Location
Vienna,
Austria
Room
Suites #300 and #400
Architect
Hans Hollein
Designer
FG Stijl
Rate
Expensive

LOCATED ON THE
PEDESTRIAN-ONLY
STEPHANSPLATZ, RIGHT
IN THE MIDDLE OF THE
MOST HISTORIC PART
OF THIS MIND-BOGGLING
HISTORIC CITY, IS
VIENNA'S DO & CO HOTEL.

DO & CO HOTEL

THE SUITES BOAST SOME
OF THE MOST AMAZING
VIEWS OF THE CATHEDERAL
AND CITY.

Its 41 luxurious rooms and 2 suites are on the sixth floor of the famous glass-walled Haas Haus building, but it is the view from the rooms that stuns. What you see is a straight-on, full-size, close-up panorama of the ornate St. Stephen's Cathedral–Stephansdom–that has defined Vienna since 1147.

Overcoming some serious challenges posed by the curved façade of the building, the Amsterdam-based design team FG Stijl has created a magical balance in the hotel's interior. The designers have managed to combine the heritage of the hotel's Istanbul-born founder, Attila Dogudan, with Vienna's prissy past and offer it all on a platform of understated luxury that still allows the views of the cathedral to remain the main attraction. While the rooms are shaped like wedges of cake, they never feel claustrophobic because of the views and the white furniture, dark teak detailing, and bare hardwood floors. The accents include colorful Turkish kilim bedspreads.

Special feature
The Onyx Bar, with vertigo-inducing views and Vienna's hippest crowd.

Can't miss
New Year's in Vienna. St. Stephen's Cathedral's massive *pummerin* (big bell) announce the arrival of the new year in Austria. Book a reservation at hotel's restaurant on the seventh floor or manhandle an invitation to a private party in DO & CO's private-event space on the eighth and ninth floors.

Although all rooms are luxurious, the most enjoyable ones are the two suites that offer the closest views of the cathedral as well as stylishly but sparsely furnished terraces overlooking Stephansplatz. If the view through the curving windows gets overwhelming, heavy curtains and sliding dark wood panels are provided to block it out. Both suites have sprawling white sofas and carpet-less hardwood floors, and this overall lack of clutter creates a feeling of lightness and ease. That sense of ease continues in the bathrooms, which are equipped with Jacuzzis, transparent showers, heated marble floors, and flat-screen TVs. Besides being fully stocked, the bar in both suites comes with an espresso machine and chocolates from the Viennese confectionary institution Demel (also owned by DO & CO), providing additional excuses to stay indoors all day.

There are subtle details everywhere to remind hotel guests of the owner's Turkish heritage, like the hand worked silvery trays that are used as side-table tops both in the Onyx bar and the rooms. At the DO & CO Hotel, it's easy to reflect back on the past while indulging in the comforts of the present.

DO & CO Hotel
Stephansplatz 12
1010 Vienna, Austria
T 43 (0) 1 24 188
F 43 (0) 1 24 188 444
www.doco.com
hotel@doco.com

Location
**Brussels,
Belgium**
Room
**The Jean-Paul Knott
Fashion Room**
Architect
Cyril Carree
Designer
Jean-Paul Knott
Rate
Expensive

A HIP STYLE AND ELEGANT ATTITUDE MAKES THIS HOTEL IDEAL FOR GUESTS WHO KNOW HOW TO MIX A LITTLE PLEASURE WITH THEIR BUSINESS.

ROYAL WINDSOR

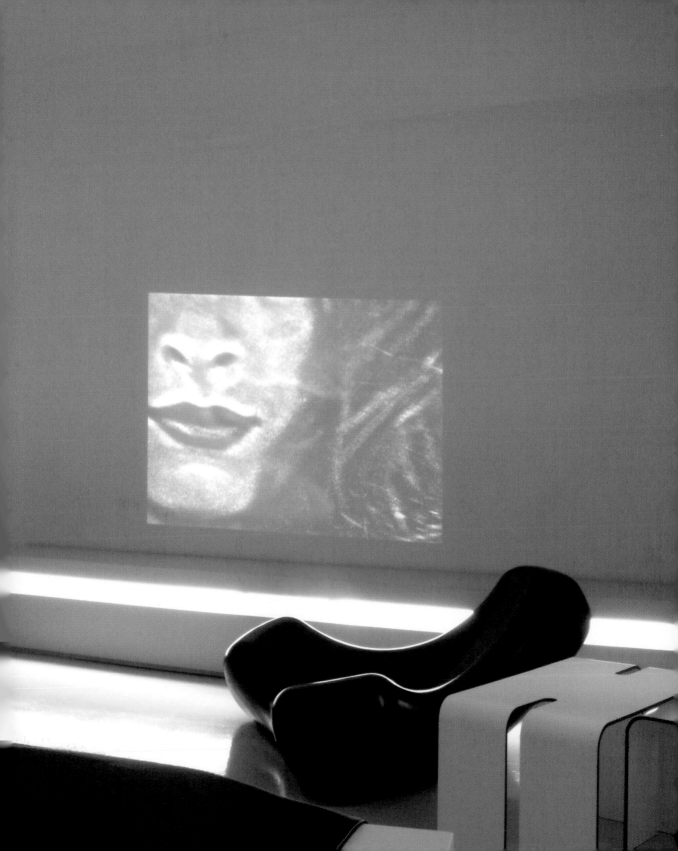

The elegant Royal Windsor Hotel Grand Place holds court in the heart of Belgium's capital. Recently refurbished, this 266-room, five-star Brussels hotel attracts a mix of young business-oriented trendsetters and tourists, making for a cosmopolitan atmosphere amid a colonial-style setting.

The attentive, personalized service of a world-class hotel is played out in the specialized décor of several rooms, each decorated by a different Belgian fashion designer. Jean-Paul Knott's Fashion Room is a spare but sophisticated room predominated by grays and soft whites, and punctuated with black leather–it's a visual extension of Knott's fashion aesthetic. The emphasis is on bareness, without being cold. Knott accomplishes warmth with his juxtaposition of contrasting textures, colours, and artful video and photo projections (pages 154 to 155). The matte gray floor is in stark contrast to the rich dark brown leather bedspread. An assortment of books, CDs, and DVDs selected by Knott himself ensure that guests are completely surrounded by his own artistic sensibilities.

Designed to match the colour of the signature Knott dessert–chocolate mousse–the room's bedspread offers decadence sans the guilt (page 157). At the Royal Windsor, grandeur is not just embellishment but, rather, necessity.

Special feature
Afternoon tea. Chutney's offers teatime everyday from 3:00 to 5:30 PM. The mouthwatering array of finger sandwiches, homemade scones, and desserts is perfectly complemented by a selection of rare teas, coffees, and cordials.

Can't miss
The market. There is nothing humble about the Grand Place, Brussels' central marketplace square with Gothic architecture.

Royal Windsor Hotel Grand Place
5 Rue Duquesnoy
1000 Brussels, Belgium
T 32 2 505 5555
F 32 2 505 5500
www.royalwindsorbrussels.com
resa.royalwindsor@warwickhotels.com

THE BEDROOM'S DÉCOR IS
A VISUAL EXTENSION OF THE
BELGIAN DESIGNER'S FASHION
AESTHETIC—A FLUID LOOK

Location
**Paphos,
Cyprus**
Room
Kyma Suite
Architect/Designer
**Joelle Pleot
and Tristan Auer**
Rate
Expensive

EVEN THE MOST JADED
COUPLE WILL GET THEIR
GROOVE BACK THANKS
TO THE ALMYRA'S
ROMANTIC SEA VIEWS
AND SECLUDED GARDENS.

ALMYRA

BREATHTAKING VIEWS
OFFER RESPITE FOR ANY
WEARIED TRAVELLER.

THE ADDED TOUCHES OF
EXTRAVAGANCE INCLUDE
TWO PRIVATE TERRACES
AND A KING-SIZED DAYBED
IN THE GARDEN.

If Aphrodite had a palace, it would be the Almyra in Paphos, the legendary birthplace of the goddess of love and beauty. Surrounded by eight acres of landscaped gardens edged by beach, with sweeping, uninterrupted views across the bay to Paphos Harbor, the hotel is a place to indulge the senses. Recent renovations on the Mediterranean beachfront have created a long swath of sugary white sand, perfect for swimming and sunbathing.

Of the hotel's 158 rooms, the one to snag is the signature Kyma Seafront Suite. Aptly named (*kyma* means "waves" in Greek), the suite is a few steps from the Mediterranean (pages 158 to 159). Situated in a lush garden, the suite features two terraces: Private rooftop terrace–candle-lit at night–that offers gorgeous views (page 160 and page 162, bottom) and ample lounge areas for retreat or entertainment, and a seafront one that includes a dining table and cream-colored sofa. A king-sized day bed, outfitted with luxurious bedding and positioned in the garden, adds an extra touch of extravagance. The glamorous tiled bathroom has a separate rainfall shower. Whether relaxing in the suite's living room (page 162, top) or going for a dip in the hotel's swimming pool (page 161), Almyra has something for everyone. Filled with natural light, the suite's design is in harmony with the surrounding outdoor beauty, making it a fit retreat for modern gods and goddesses.

Special feature

Kid-friendly atmosphere. Almyra features a children's club and kids-only menus. Parents using the Baby Go Lightly service can order every manner of baby item online in advance, saving space in their luggage. One of the fresh water pools is especially designed for children.

Can't miss

The archaeology. A short walk from the hotel in the old town of Paphos is the house of Dionysus, a Roman villa dating back to the second century.

Almyra
Poseidonos Avenue
8042 Paphos, Cyprus
T 357 26 888 700
F 357 26 942 818
www.almyra.com
almyra@thanoshotels.com

Location
**Copenhagen,
Denmark**
Room
#106 and #206
Architect/Designer
**Geneviève Gauckler #106
and WK Interact #206**
Rate
Moderate

FROM THE MOMENT GUESTS STEP INTO ANY ONE OF THE HOTEL'S 61 ROOMS, THEY'RE GUARANTEED AN OUT-OF-THIS-WORLD EXPERIENCE.

HOTEL FOX

THE WALL PAINTING OF THE
PJ HARVEY LOOK-ALIKE WAS
DESIGNED TO LOOK LIKE
A FLIP BOOK IN MOTION.

THE ROOMS HAVE
BEEN CREATED BY
GRAPHIC DESIGNERS,
URBAN ARTISTS
AND ILLUSTRATORS.

To launch one of its cars, Volkswagon commissioned 21 international graphic designers, graffiti artists, illustrators, and all-around trendsetters to renovate the 61-room Hotel Fox. The result is 61 individualized pieces of art that encompass everything from Japanese manga to old-school graffiti to futuristic designs (pages 164 to 165, 168 to 169, and 171). While there are only 17 XL-sized rooms, there's no shortage of imagination in this designer-friendly playground.

Two standouts, rooms 106 and 206, are delightfully quirky (pages 166 to 167). Designed by French artist Geneviève Gauckler, room 106 is all about fun all the time. She describes it as being the "glorious, Technicolor-dream-coat room where rocking horse people eat marshmallow pies." And, indeed, one night spent here is akin to slipping inside the Wonka factory. The room is a jolt of just-right sweetness with its vivid cotton-candy colors and playful graphics.

On the other end of the spectrum is room 206, by French artist WK Interact, who designed the room to be "like a flip book in motion." There's a black-and-white wall painting in the eerie likeness of cult crooner PJ Harvey, and depending on where one walks or stands in the room, the painting seems to move, too. The bathroom in the room—and those throughout the hotel—is utilitarian and resembles one found in a college dorm, which makes it acceptably ironic.

The VW Fox supermini may have never made it stateside, but Hotel Fox is a perfectly cool substitute for any expat.

Special feature
Check in. Guests are given one of three options: The Lover Bag, filled with champagne and chocolates; the Movie Bag, filled with beer and popcorn; or the Hangover Bag, filled with Bloody Mary makings and aspirin.

Can't miss
The kitchen and bar. The food is seriously innovative and healthy—all ingredients are Nordic and free-range. There's a recommended cocktail for each course. Try the Glitterati: Gin, rose syrup, and champagne.

Hotel Fox
Jarmers Plads 3
DK-1551 Copenhagen V, Denmark
T 45 33 95 77 55
F 45 33 14 30 33
www.hotelfox.dk
hotel@hotelfox.dk

THE HOTEL WAS
COMMISSIONED
BY VOLKSWAGEN
TO CELEBRATE
THE LAUNCH OF
ONE ITS CARS.

Location
**Paris,
France**
Room
**Hats and Poems
and the Vitrine**
Architect/Designer
**Morgane Rousseau,
Fréderic Comtet,
and Mathieu Paillard**
Rate
Expensive

HIDDEN FROM PLAIN VIEW,
HOTEL PARTICULIER IS LIKE
AN R-RATED, OH-SO-PRIVATE
PLAYGROUND WITH A TOUCH
OF PARISIAN CHARM.

HOTEL PARTICULIER

THIS HOTEL EXUDES ELEGANCE, INTIMACY, AND FASHION.

TO GET TO THE HOTEL,
GUESTS MUST FIRST
FIND THE TREE-SHROUDED
SECRET PATH.

**ONE ROOM FEATURES
A TURKISH BATH AND
A CABINET FULL OF
EROTIC KNICKKNACKS,**

In order to find Hotel Particulier Montmartre, start thinking like former Montmartre resident Salvador Dalí and find the tree-shrouded secret pathway between avenue Junot and rue Lepic that leads to a large black gate. Behind this imposing gateway lies the mansion-cum-hotel, surrounded by a beautiful garden and comprised of just five suites. Each suite was conceptualized by a French artist and must be experienced, one by one, to be believed. But two rooms do stand out from the rest based purely on their sense of eccentric humor and tasteful design: The Hats and Poems Room (pages 172 to 173) and the Vitrine Room (page 175).

Olivier Saillard designed the Hats and Poems Room. Known for creating events at the Fashion Musuem in Paris, Saillard's room is subtly whimsical. Hanging from every object and piece of furniture is a small envelope meant to look like a price tag, the contents of which reveal a poem. The décor of the room itself is simplicity at its most black-and-white basic. The white walls and white bed are offset by black nightstands and black lamps, which have hats for shades. Glossy black tiles give the bathroom a chic uniformity. Pleasantly serene, the room is fashionable in an effortless, Parisian way.

Special feature
Le petit salon de lecture (the reading room). There are over 1,000 titles on everything from fashion to music. The owners gathered the books while they were working in the art and film industries.

Can't miss
The furniture collection. The reading room's furniture is a designer's dream, featuring first editions of Arne Jacobsen's Egg chair and Mies van der Rohe's Barcelona chair.

Painter and sculptor Philippe Mayaux, winner of the Marcel Duchamp Prize in 2006, designed the Vitrine Room, and the room certainly appears as though Duchamp had a hand in creating it. The room features a wild assortment of exotic accessories, like an erotically charged nineteenth-century *cabinet des curiosités* that includes tiny lips, a pink glass mollusklike creature, and a miniscule baby doll suspended in a glass ball. Beyond these eclectic flourishes, the décor of the bedroom is unassuming, awash in butter-colored walls and soft lighting. The Vitrine Room has one special feature that the other rooms lack: a private Turkish bath and an all-mirrored wall, making it irresistibly extraordinaire.

Want to sample all the rooms at once? The entire hotel can be rented in its totality for a single stay. Then everyone will find the room that's just right—until it's time to switch.

Hotel Particulier Montmartre
23, avenue Junot
75018 Paris, France
T 33 (0)1 53 41 81 40
www.hotel-particulier-montmartre.com

Location
**Berlin,
Germany**
Room
Premium Suite
Architect
Guiliana Salmaso
Designer
Goetz Maximilian Keller
Rate
Moderate

LOCATED IN BERLIN'S
ENERGETIC AND HIP
CENTRAL DISTRICT
OF MITTE, THE HOTEL
IS SURROUNDED BY
CHIC FASHION SHOPS,
GALLERIES, AND TRENDY
PLACES TO EAT.

LUX 11

SET IN WHAT IS
ORIGINALLY A LATE
NINETEENTH-CENTURY
RESIDENTIAL BUILDING,
THIS BOUTIQUE HOTEL

GREAT LOCATION—
EVERYTHING COOL
OR TOURISTY IN
BERLIN IS WITHIN
A SHORT DISTANCE.

Located in the historic Mitte district, Lux 11 is right at home among the designer boutiques, art galleries, and refurbished buildings–a perfect setting for the modern vibe that Lux 11 imparts. Set in what was originally a late nineteenth-century residential building, the 72-room boutique hotel is affordably chic. The ground floor is mainly occupied by the hotel's salon and spa, the all-white Shiro i Shiro restaurant, and a micro-department fashion store.

The small reception area and lack of round-the-clock service signals the fact that this is a hotel for low-maintenance guests desiring a DIY, apartment-like setting. Guests stay here for its primo location–everything cool or touristy in Berlin is within steps of Lux 11–and its no-nonsense approach to design. Since the guestrooms are quite small, it makes sense to upgrade to the more spacious Premium Suite.

Beyond its sleek interiors and cream-colored walls, the suite boasts a terrace and a fully equipped kitchen stocked with every kind of cooking appliance. (Not that one should ever dare spend a night cooking while the delicious Shiro i Shiro beckons below, but for the epicurean traveler, the kitchen is an added bonus.) Lichen-colored polished concrete flooring, which sometimes alternates with bleached wood, forms the basis for the suite's open floor plan. The bedroom's suede headboard and its taffeta bedcover trimmed with fake fur provide wonderful tactile sensations amid the rest of the suite's cool exuberance. Unlike the rest of the guestrooms, the Premier Suite offers an ample-sized bathtub accessible via smooth concrete steps. Placed in the center of the washroom, the bath sets the tone for tranquil relaxation. A porcelain sink atop a concrete block appears more as a study in design simplicity than as a functional basin. Happily, form follows function here.

Much like SoHo in New York City used to be–before artist's spaces turned into retail shops–there is an enthusiastic energy that enlivens the Mitte district. Lux 11 retains the independence of the traditional German spirit while acting as a harbinger of change.

Special feature
The spa. While an Aveda salon and spa may be old hat to big city travelers, it's a welcome and much-needed addition to Mitte. It's popular, too, so book a day in advance.

Can't miss
Ulf Haines.
This micro-department store sells high fashion clothes and gear, and is located adjacent to the hotel lobby. It's run by a former buyer for Quartier 206, one of Berlin's poshest fashion emporiums.

Lux 11
Rosa-Luxemburg-Strasse 9–13
D-101788 Berlin, Germany
T 49 (0)30 93 62 80 0
F 49 (0)30 93 62 80 80
www.lux-eleven.com
info@lux-eleven.com

Location
**Frankfurt,
Germany**
Room
Russisch Brot
Architect
**Alexander Bernjus
and Hathumar Gisbertz**
Designer
**Delphine Buhro
and Michael Dreher**
Rate
Moderate

WITH THEIR QUIRKY
SENSIBILITY AND DÉCOR,
THE ROOMS AT THE GOLDMAN
25 HOURS ARE SURE TO
ENCOURAGE EVERYONE'S
PLAYFUL SIDE.

GOLDMAN 25HOURS

The eye-catching orange-and-blue façade of Goldman 25hours Hotel hints at the colorful exuberance that permeates each of the 49 guestrooms on its seven thematically colored floors. Each room is individually themed. A room decorated in the style and flair of 1890s Paris fronts another devoted to the words and wisdom of the 1950s poets. Still another is done up to reflect the glitter and glitz of a casino. Other rooms are set apart by various whimsal decorations and declarations–*Schokolade macht nicht dick* ("Chocolate doesn't make you fat") and *Grün ist die liebe* ("Love is green"), for example–written on the walls. Choosing a favorite among so many design-conscious rooms is difficult, especially given that apart from identical basic made-to-measure furniture, they have different accessories and decorations collected from designers all over Europe. However, there is one room that pleasantly stands out among the rest: Russisch Brot, which means Russian bread (page 189).

This blazing red room features a ruby-colored carpet and flamboyant vintage lamps; instead of wallpaper, there are ornamental paintings and quotes printed on the walls that play upon the name of the room. Russisch Brot refers to popular cookies shaped like letters of the alphabet.

Children (and childlike adults) like to create strings of nonsensical words before eating them. The text above the bed, for instance, tells the romantically intricate story of the letters A and B, who meet in an erotic novel. Situated on the fourth floor–where everything from floor to ceiling is red–this room may be just the right backdrop for a bit of guest-inspired romance, too.

Frankfurt's East End is eclectically energetic, a place where high-end avante-garde intersects with mainstream pop culture, and Goldman 25hours keenly synthesizes the surrounding environment into a place of extreme comfort and style. Here, even kitsch comes off as being consciously hip: The hotel living room's stiff green armchairs may be protected by white crocheted doilies (page 186 to 187), but the über-cool pink-and-pale-green lighting fixtures and the private terrace offset any possibility that this is Hansel and Gretel's place.

Special feature
The tech hookup. All rooms come equipped with their own listening dock for iPods; iPods can be borrowed from the reception.

Can't miss
The Goldman Restaurant. The chef combines the cuisine of Germany and France, making the menu, which changes monthly, one of the city's most innovative.

Goldman 25hours Hotel
Hanauer Landstraße 127
60314 Frankfurt, Germany
T 49 (0) 69 405 86 89 0
F 49 (0) 69 405 86 89 890
www.25hours-frankfurt.de
frankfurt@25hours-hotels.com

SOME ROOMS ARE SET
APART BY VARIOUS
DECLARATIONS WRITTEN
ON THE WALL, LIKE
"LOVE IS GREEN," WHILE
ANOTHER TELLS THE
EROTICALLY INTRICATE
STORY OF A AND B.

Location
Athens, Greece
Room
Penthouse Suite
Architect
Kyriakides Associates S.A.
Designer
Karim Rashid
Rate
Expensive

THE HOTEL'S FREE-FORM SWIMMING POOL DAZZLES WITH ITS KITSCHY COMBINATION OF COLORFUL TILES.

SEMIRAMIS

THE ROOM'S FLASHY
PALETTE INDUCES A FEEL-
GOOD GIDDINESS THAT
RIVALS WILLY WONKA'S
CANDY-COLORED WORLD.

TECHNOLOGY REIGNS
SUPREME IN THIS HOTEL,
WHERE GUESTS USE LEDS
TO POST MESSAGES ON
THEIR DOOR.

Situated in the leafy Kifissia area of north Athens, high enough to avoid the city's humidity, the 52-room Semiramis is a hotel of the future that realizes the vision of Egyptian-British designer Karim Rashid. Known for his fluid style and bold use of color, Rashid explains his point of view on hotel design: "Hotels today make you feel like you're living in the previous century. That's the last thing I wanted to do."

Avoiding the stuffy and old-fashioned, Rashid designed every element for Semiramis, from its swimming pool to the staff's uniforms. The exterior is covered in small, glossy white ceramic tiles. Guests enter through a glowing pink glass cube into a spacious lobby where glass walls change colors and radiate with subtle motion. A rotating collection of art includes works by Tim Noble, Sue Webster, and Jeff Koons. This backdrop is the perfect setting for Rashid's signature furniture, including his Wavelength sofa, Swing chair, and a bank of black sofas shaped like pouting lips. Instead of numbers, the rooms are identified by Rashid-designed symbols, reminiscent of modern hieroglyphics.

The best room in the house is the Penthouse Suite (pages 192, left and page 194, left). Situated on the hotel's roof, two of the suite's four walls are made entirely of glass—ideal for exhibitionists or anyone who, more sheepishly, just wants to soak in the stellar sights of the entire region. Rashid's handiwork is everywhere—from the suite's backlit headboards to the slippers under the bed to the placemats that dot the tables. Featuring furniture done up in bubblegum pink or bright lime green, Rashid uses the Starburst-inspired palette to add warmth to the otherwise sparse environment and white epoxy floors. The frosted glass bathroom gets a little glitz with the silver encrusted bathtub that resembles a disco ball (page 194, right). Even the closets have been designed with curved corners.

In the modern world of Semiramis, technology reigns supreme. Video projection, holopro glass technology, dot matrix LEDs, and other digital projection media can be found throughout the hotel and in the suite. Guests can use scrolling LEDs to post messages on their door– "privacy" or "please make up room," or more provocatively, "Hello, I'm single. Please come in." Never before has technology been so practical and comfortable, making the Semiramis an icon of inspirational high-design.

Special feature

The views. The Penthouse Suite isn't located on the rooftop for nothing (page 193).

Can't miss

The rotating collection of fine art on the main floor. Semiramis, commissioned by Greek industrialist and art patron Dakis Joannou, reflects his dedication to the art world.

Semiramis
48 Charilaou Trikoupi Str.
145 62 Kefalari-Kifissia
Athens, Greece
T 30 210 62 84 400
F 30 210 62 84 499
www.semiramisathens.com and
www.yeshotels.gr
info@semiramisathens.com

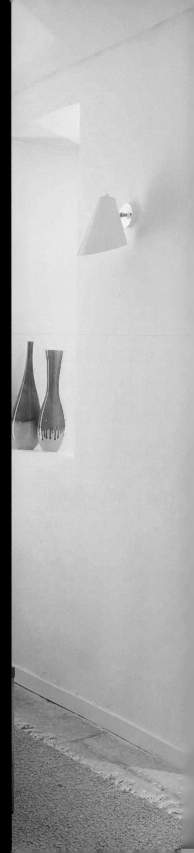

Location
Mykonos, Greece
Room
Junior Suite
Architect
Yiannis Tsimas
Designer
Angelos Angelopoulos
Rate
Expensive

A NIGHT'S STAY AT THIS HOTEL IS THE BEST WAY TO INDULGE ONE'S VISIONS OF LUXURY.

MYKONOS THEOXENIA

For over 40 years, the Mykonos Theoxenia has ranked among the top cosmopolitan locations on the Aegean. Built on the seafront amid landscaped gardens, the low-rise structure with 52 rooms overlooks the island's landmark white windmills and bay. The vibrant, glamorous nightlife of the town of Mykonos is only a stroll away.

The hotel's original designer was renowned architect Aris Costantinides, who incorporated local stone and traditional architecture on the exterior while decorating the interior in 1960s pop style (page 199, bottom right). The hotel's revamp in 2004 by Yiannis Tsimas and Angelos Angelopoulos stayed true to Costantinides' original vision. They kept the 1960s glam style yet brought the hotel up to contemporary standards, including adding a freeform swimming pool surrounded by gardens (page 199, bottom left).

The Junior Suite revels in 1960s décor (pages 196 to 197 and 199, top). Retro lamps and chairs—in a candy-color assortment of bright lime, tangerine, and cherry—are kitsch done right. Stone-clad walls, hessian fabrics, and minimal surfaces form a backdrop for sleek sofas. Retro period furniture made of light beech wood grounds the room's over-the-top color scheme. The suite's floor is made from local blue-gray stone. Through the opened windows, the breezes from the Aegean Sea sweep the spacious bedroom and an open-plan living room that leads to a veranda with a pergola—a fantastic setting for a romantic dinner. Smoked-glass walls enclose a white bathroom, which is filled with products, including his-and-her slippers—a reminder that serenity can also be hip.

The redesign and refurbishing of Mykonos Theoxenia has elevated this Greek island to the status of a sophisticated retreat. In its former heyday, the hotel attracted the ultraglitterati, including Jackie and Aristotle Onassis. Now, once again, the jet set has begun to sashay up the runway-style drive, which is spectacular when floodlit at night.

Special feature
Outstanding service worthy of a shipping tycoon or an heiress. The hotel has a heliport, and the accommodating staff is at the ready to rent a car, a boat, or even a Lear jet for guests.

Can't miss
Sundowners at the Breeze In and Breeze Out bars during sunset.

Mykonos Theoxenia
84600 Kato Mili
Mykonos, Greece
T 30 22890 22230
F 30 22890 23008
www.mykonostheoxenia.com
info@mykonostheoxenia.com

JACKIE AND ARISTOTLE
ONASSIS STAYED HERE
IN THE HOTEL'S HEYDAY,
WHICH STILL RETAINS
ITS AURA OF 1960S
GLAM STYLE.

Location
Santorini,
Greece
Room
Winemaker House
Architect/Designer
Akis Charalambous
Rate
Expensive

WITH COMMANDING
VIEWS OVER SANTORINI,
THE CALDERA, AND THE
CYCLADIC GREEK ISLANDS,
THE IKIES IS THE ULTIMATE
ROMANTIC GETAWAY.

IKIES

A HONEYMOON SUITE LIKE NO
OTHER, THE WINEMAKER HOUSE
IS AT ONCE ELEGANT, REFINED,
AND LAID-BACK IN STYLE.

Architecturally inspired by the traditional local houses that are carved out of pumice stone, Ikies Traditional Houses are designed to make its guests feel like locals. The 11 houses that make up the hotel's complex are perched on separate levels of the caldera, ensuring individually breathtaking views of the surrounding volcanic islets. Each house is named after a profession associated with Santorini—from carpenter to captain to everyone's favorite, winemaker. The simple furnishings of each house are punctuated with artwork and objects from each profession.

Technically considered a honeymoon suite, the Winemaker House has romantic views, a cozy atmosphere, and complimentary champagne brunches that are served on the terrace that will appeal to anybody, newlywed or not. The room's design style is simple and takes its cues from the colors of the landscape—white, cerulean, and sand. Furniture is sparse and comfortable; nothing is over-the-top here, except perhaps the amenities, which include a secluded terrace with uninterrupted views and a private hot tub atop a spacious teak deck (pages 200 to 201). The fully tiled bathroom comes complete with a Jacuzzi*, a steam room, and a walk-in shower (page 202, bottom right).

Perhaps the most unique feature of the Winemaker's house is its master bedroom (page 202, bottom left). Built into a cave that has been carved out of pumice rock, the bedroom is simple and elegant. Tucked into the alcove, the all-white bed's mattress is made of natural materials, like sea grass, horsehair, and coconut, which prove surprisingly comfortable. Lamps are set into small nooks next to the bed's headboard. A well-equipped kitchen and separate living areas with two sofas and a dining table round out the Winemaker.

True to its name, the Winemaker House is decorated in a vintner's motif. Sepia-toned photographs of the region's vineyards dot the walls. The vaulted ceiling gives the effect of standing inside an elaborate wine cellar. Baskets used to carry grapes line the terrace walls while large jugs and bottle decorate the bedroom's armoire. The house's centerpiece is the antique winery vat.

A haven for travelers looking for a unique experience amid a breathtaking environment, the Ikies is sure to inspire the most jaded guest to embrace the lighter side of life.

Special feature
The sunsets. As guests watch the sun set over the Aegean Sea, the discreet staff will happily serve sundowners on the terrace (page 202, top).

Can't miss
The Sigalas Winery. Located across the street from the hotel, the winery is a favorite among locals. Order a few plates of mezes—Santorini cheeses, bread salad, and cod with sun-dried tomatoes and capers—to pair with the wine.

Ikies Traditional Houses
Oia, Santorini
84702 Cyclades Greece
T 30 22 860 71 311
F 30 22 860 71 953
www.ikies.com
info@ikies.com

SETTING THE STANDARD FOR ROYAL TREATMENT, THE NEW YORK PALACE HAS EXPERTLY IMPORTED THE SPIRIT OF NYC INTO THE OLD-WORLD GRANDEUR OF BUDAPEST.

NEW YORK PALACE HOTEL

IT'S THE SHOCK
OF THE NEW MEETS
OLD, AS EXEMPLIFIED
BY THE TURQUOISE
MURANO CHANDELIER
IN THE ROYAL SUITE.

When the majestic New York Palace Hotel was built in 1894, its architectural style reflected baroque and Italian Renaissance influences (page 209, left). Located in the heart of Budapest, the building's lavish interiors– filled with Venetian antiques, marble, and miles of silk and velvet curtains–evoked comparisons to the palace of the Bavarian King Louis II. The New York Café, a charming bistro still open today, attracted intellectuals and artists like Sir Alexander Korda and Michael Curtis, the Oscar-winning director of *Casablanca*.

When the Italian Boscolo Group undertook a renovation of the legendary 112-room hotel, the group strove to preserve its period styles as much as possible but updated the guestrooms to create a more modern look. The building still features high-quality materials, including Italian marble. Opulence abounds, from the bronze statues that decorate the building's public spaces to the original panel paintings that adorn the walls and ceilings.

Special feature

The Spa and Wellness Center. Brilliantly designed, the spa was inspired by an alpine ice tunnel to provide total relaxation amid waterfalls, digital images of colored ice, and Swarovski crystal prisms. Above the indoor pool, the ceiling is set with tiny blue LEDs to represent the sky.

Can't miss

The Cigar Bar (page 204 to 205). Guests can meditate and relax over cognac while enjoying the aroma of fine cigars, which are kept in old bank safes used as humidors.

While every guestroom feels regal, the most exquisite is the Royal Suite.

Decorated with gilded mirrors, muted gold fabrics, handwoven silk wallpaper, and vases of freshly cut pale yellow roses, it is the epitome of elegance. A delicate turquoise-colored Murano chandelier reflects the refinement of a bygone era while its shocking hue enlivens the room with a more contemporary sensibility (pages 206 to 207). The juxtaposition between old-world Italian flair and modern design speaks to the hotel's overall eccentric style. The suite's decadent marble bathroom and corner tub, for example, is updated with a separate glass-walled shower. Perhaps the best feature of the suite, however, is the view from its private and spacious balcony (page 209, right). Overlooking the city, it's easy to envision life as one of the royals.

The New York Palace combines the intellectual café life of New York City with the romance and grandeur of old Italy with accents of contemporary design, all in the bustling city of Budapest.

New York Palace Hotel
Erzsébet krt. 9-11
1073 Budapest, Hungary
T 36 1 8866 111
F 36 1 8866 199
www.boscolohotels.com
reservation@newyork.boscolo.com

AS OPULENT ON THE
OUTSIDE AS IT IS ON
THE INSIDE, THE HOTEL

Location
**Florence,
Italy**
Room
Penthouse Consorti
Architect/Designer
Michele Bönan
Rate
Expensive

IN FLORENCE ONE BECOMES NEWLY AWARE OF ONE'S SURROUNDINGS—THE SEAMLESS FUSION OF ANCIENT WITH MODERN.

CONTINENTALE

THE HOTEL USES THE
HIGHEST-QUALITY
MATERIALS AND HAS
IMPECCABLE DETAILS
OF CRAFTSMANSHIP.

GUESTS CAN WATCH THE
BUSTLING ACTIVITY ON
THE PONTE VECCHIO FROM
THE ROOFTOP TERRACE.

The perfect way to contemplate all this is to indulge in a soak in the sleek, king-sized tub in the loft-level bathroom of the Penthouse Consorti at the Continentale—the continental pleasing hotel owned |by the Salvatore Ferragamo luxury goods empire. (Yes, *that* Ferragamo, the man who designed all those shoes.) As one marvels at the simple elegance of the stark bathtub, with the magnificent view of the Ponte Vecchio over the river Arno is at one's blissful disposal. In addition to the sexy bath and breathtaking views, the bathroom offers double showers and an LCD TV (one of two in the suite).

At the entrance level of the duplex Penthouse Suite there's a large bed covered by a canopy of feather-light white drapes (page 210 to 211). The bed linen, cushions, sofas, armchairs, and lampshades are also all white, as are the floor-to ceiling curtains that cover the windows. (Want to feel completely enveloped in white, airy luxury? Draw the curtains and let the bed canopy out.) A fully furnished private terrace, the highest-quality materials, and impeccable details of craftsmanship in the furnishings round out the suite's amenities and express the old-world-meets-new design vibes of the hotel (pages 212 to 214). This is the only large suite in the 43-room hotel, so be sure to reserve it in advance.

Continentale is considered to be the crown jewel of Ferragamo's nine hotels. Its interior designer, Michele Bönan, has found a balance between the fourteenth-century heritage of the building, a 1950s bubblegum vibe in homage to the heyday of Italian style, and a high-tech sensibility. As a nod to all these influences, heavy drapery, pink and pistachio accents, and a multimedia show greet guests in the lobby, but the theme is light-handed and never steps over the line.

Special feature
The rooftop terrace. Guests can sip their martinis on white-canvas chaise lounges while enjoying the stunning 360-degree views across the Florentine skyline and surrounding hills.

Can't miss
The Lungarno Details store just across the street. The shop sells impeccable examples of style and design—from bath and bedroom accessories to books and collectibles.

Continentale
Vicolo dell'Oro, 6r
50123 Florence, Italy
T 39 055 2726 4000
www.lungarnohotels.com
bookings@lungarnohotels.com

Location
**Florence,
Italy**
Room
Suite #4
Architect/Designer
Claudio Nardi
Rate
Expensive

VIVA THE RIVA. A FAMILY-RUN OPERATION, THE HOTEL OFFERS THE COMFORT OF A QUAINT B&B WITH THE COSMOPOLITANISM OF A WORLD-CLASS BOUTIQUE.

RIVA LOFTS

ARCHED WINDOWS
IMBUE THE ROOM
WITH A FEELING
OF SPACIOUSNESS

KNOLL-DESIGNED WHITE
SOFAS, COWHIDE RUGS,
OVERSIZED LAMPS, AND
MIRRORS MAKES FOR AN
ELECTIC COMBINATION.

A 20-minute walk from Florence, the Riva Lofts looks like a charming Tuscan hamlet surrounded by green. Built in the nineteenth century as a factory, then transformed into artisans' workshops, this small complex of stone buildings served as the architecture studio of Claudio Nardi, known for his high-fashion boutiques for Dolce & Gabbana. Along with his well-traveled daughter Alice, Nardi refurbished the buildings to create avant-garde guest residences.

While preserving much of the original materials and spacious design, the Nardis have chosen sleek and modern furnishings. Several Mies van der Rohe-designed armchairs and a polished tropical wood table designed by Nardi stand against a raw stone wall. The big hall with stone walls, a cross vault, bookshelves, and fireplace has large windows that overlook the private garden and a spectacular swimming pool of white sandstone. Guests gather in the garden for breakfast and conversation. The hotel's meeting room has the same comfortable but elegant feel.

The nine suites—each with a separate entrance—were designed in the spirit of French studios, combining metropolitan style with a cozy, domestic atmosphere. Of the nine suites, Suite 4 is loftlike in scope and features three floors (pages 216 to 223). A little known fact: Claudio Nardi lived in here until 2004. It has a beautiful view of the Arno, the Parco delle Cascine, and Brunelleschi's Dome from its living room, making it primo hotel real estate. The eclectic combination of furniture includes Knoll-designed white sofas, cowhide rugs, oversized lamps, and mirrors. There is a kitchen with walnut wood counters; the all-white bedroom has a remote-controlled skylight and a concealed peephole in the wall, so the same view from the living room can be seen from the bedroom, too.

The Riva, which opened in 2006, attracts the international art set. "We've already had several art exhibitions and design-related events," says Alice. "And then, of course, there are all my father's architecture friends. It's been a full house almost since the beginning."

Special feature

The transportation. In keeping with the friendly, easygoing atmosphere at Riva, guests are provided with bicycles to get around town.

Can't miss

A tour of the Oltarno. This is a lesser-known part of Florence on the south bank where all the locals go to take in Santo Spirito and San Frediano, the Boboli gardens, and lively artisans' shops and restaurants. Visit Quelle Tre for the latest in women's fashions or Stefano Bremer's shop for handmade shoes.

Riva Lofts
Via Baccio Bandinelli 98,
50142 Florence, Italy
T 39 055 7130272
F 39 055 711103
www.rivahotel.it
info@rivahotel.it

ANY ROOM IN THE LOFT
LIKE SUITE GIVES GUESTS
A STUNNING VIEW OF
THE RIVER ARNO AND
BRUNELLESCHI'S DOME.

Location
Lana,
Italy
Room
Suite
Architect
Matteo Thun
Designer
Matteo Thun
and Partners
Rate
Expensive

THE RESORT'S INNATE SENSE OF BALANCE IS REVOLUTIONIZING THE WAY HOTELIERS ARE GOING GREEN.

VIGILIUS MOUNTAIN

SURROUNDED BY NATURAL
GRANDUER, THE TRUE VISION
OF PEACE LIES WITHIN.

IT'S ALL ABOUT NATURE
HERE. EVEN THE WATER
FROM THE POOL COMES
FROM A NEARBY SPRING.

Accessible only by a seven-minute cable car ride up the side of Vigiljoch Mountain near Merano, the Vigilius Mountain Resort stretches across a ridge, undisturbed by roads, traffic, or noise (page 224 to 225). The architect Matteo Thun used only local materials, and his technique of combining the old–300-year-old timber beams, for example–and state-of-the art materials illustrates the resort's commitment to renewable resources. The grass growing on the roof is more than a design aesthetic; it is an ecological solution to energy conservation. The resort has a carbon dioxide neutral heating system that burns wood chips.

This eco-friendly theme is further played out in the 41 guestrooms, including the spacious Suite, which feature heated clay-dividing walls and partitions that provide cozy warmth in the bedroom (page 226 and 228, left) and bathrooms (pages 227). Decorated with natural materials, like larch wood, and warm colors, the suite's floor-to-ceiling windows lead to an ample-sized balcony so guests can take in the views of the Dolomites, which are almost always visible because the sun shines 300 days a year here.

The sitting area beckons with a comfortable sofa; a fireplace; a handwoven, paprika-colored carpet; and rustic yet hip furnishing mingled with Tyrolean antiques, like the huge wardrobe (page 228, right). The bathroom offers another panoramic look at the mountains. The effect of this simple décor is to inspire guests to enjoy the outdoors–the resort's main attraction. The hotel offers the usual luxury amenities, but a TV and DVD are available only on request, another detail that makes for a distraction-free stay.

The Vigilius Mountain Resort is the ultimate escape. The air is laden with the invigorating scent of pine and greenery. Though surrounded by natural grandeur, the true vision of peace lies within, and Vigilius just makes it a tad easier to attain.

Special feature
Outdoor fun. The resort offers free archery lessons and has mountain bikes, snow-shoes, and toboggans. The Xtreme Team will facilitate hiking tours or paragliding over the surrounding villages. For a tour of the local vineyards, the staff will arrange to hire a Ferrari.

Can't miss
The infinity pool in the spa. Lined with quartz, the pool is flanked by a wall of windows that showcase the area's surrounding natural beauty and give guests the sensation of swimming into the mountains.

Vigilius Mountain Resort
Vigiljoch Mountain
I-39011 Lana, Italy
T 39 0473 556 600
F 39 0473 556 699
www.vigilius.it
info@vigilius.it

Location
**Milan,
Italy**
Room
Suite
Room no.
Suite #604
Architect/Designer
Vincenzo de Cotiis
Rate
Expensive

DECORATED WITH
A DISTINCTLY ITALIAN FLAIR
FOR FASHION, THE STRAF
HAS MADE A NAME FOR ITSELF
AS A STYLE COGNOSCENTE.

STRAF

THE LIGHTING AND
TEXTURES IMBUE IT
WITH A SUPRISINGLY
WARM ATMOSPHERE.

Located amid Milan's busy streets and surrounded by landmark architecture, the Straf hotel has such intimidating neighbors as the Duomo and La Scala opera house. It holds its own, however, as the new kid on the block. While its façade dates from the 1880s, its interior is modern, making the hotel an attraction for forward-thinking guests like Moby, John Malkovitch, and Jeff Koons (page 235).

Working in collaboration with the owners, fashion designer Vincenzo de Cotiis, known for his use of recycled and vintage materials, utilized a similar sensibility to create the Straf's dramatic interiors. Using such elements as polished concrete, burnished brass, iron, and pieces of gauze slipped behind plates of glass, de Cotiis created an austere and industrial aesethic. It's high-tech and functional, but the lighting and textures imbue it with a surprisingly warm atmosphere.

Special feature
The well-being rooms. Outfitted with a Japanese massage chair, these rooms offer the latest in chromotherapy and aromatherapy.

Can't miss
The Straf bar. Here minimalism is tossed out the door in favor of overdecoration, including a green Plexiglas® chandelier from the 1970s and brown patchwork-leather sofas.

Suite 604, located on the top floor, is the largest of the 64 guestrooms, but forgoes over-the-top décor in favor of a more hard-edged, clean sensibility (pages 230 to 231). The sprawling suite has hosted fashion shows by a coterie of young designers like Viktor & Rolf attracted to the novelty of the innovative use of raw materials—corrugated ceilings, cement walls, black slate-stone baths, and shimmering copper paneling. Don't be fooled, though: De Cotiis takes comfort seriously and uses gauzy curtains, lots of mirrors, and deep reds and earthy browns to soften the look. Colorful artwork by de Cotiis hung above a vibrant red couch bestows a feeling of intimacy. The two rooms have generous windows, two private balconies overlooking the Duomo, and loads of natural light, which further enhances the feeling of spaciousness.

Slang for St. Rafael, Straf gives Italian traditionalism a run for its money—and sets a new standard for the luxe lifestyle.

Straf
Via San Raffaele 3
20121 Milan, Italy
T 39 02 805081
F 39 02 89095294
www.straf.it
info@straf.it

THE SUITE HAS HOSTED
FASHION SHOWS BY
YOUNG DESIGNERS
LIKE VIKTOR & ROLF.

Location
Verona,
Italy
Room
Mendini Island Junior Suite
and Presidential Suite
Architect/Designer
Alessandro Mendini
Rate
Expensive

THE ART COLLECTION IN
THIS HOTEL IS IMPRESSIVE
ENOUGH TO MAKE THE
MOST KNOWLEDGEABLE
BUYER SWOON.

BYBLOS ART HOTEL

THE ATTENTION
TO HIGH-END DESIGN
SHOWS IN THE TILED
BATHROOM AND
THE PHILIPPE STARCK

GUESTS ARE IMMERSED IN
A QUIRKY, COLORFUL GALLERY
OF ART THE INSTANT THEY STEP
INSIDE THE ANTIQUE VILLA.

Byblos, already a household name as a fashion brand, owns the art-laden Byblos Art Hotel Villa Amista on a hill in Corrubbio, just a few miles from the center of Verona. Conceived as both an art gallery and a hotel, the rooms immerse guests in colorful and quirky design from the instant they step inside the otherwise antique villa.

Brainchild of Byblos owner and contemporary art enthusiast Dino Facchini, the hotel plays host not only to travelers but to works of art by a laundry list of creative heavyweights, including Takashi Murakami, Vanessa Beecroft, Cindy Sherman, and Kimsooja, whose works decorate the walls and hallways of the ornate, 70-room baroque villa.

This neo-baroque splendor is best experienced in the hotel's two most distinctive suites: the Mendini Island Junior Suite (pages 238 to 239 and page 240) and the Presidential Suite (pages 236 to 237).

Special feature

The art. Byblos is an art gallery acting as a hotel. Here's a chance to get up close to great work by respected and innovative artists.

Can't miss

The wine cellar. With a vaulted ceiling that dates from the fifteenth century, the cellar is a beauty in its own right, and there are over 300 different labels of wines to sample.

A chromatic playground of sorts, the Island Junior Suite features bright yellow, peach, and orange walls separated by large mirrors cobbled together with smaller pieces of glass. Primary colors are pixilated into tiled mosaics that make up part of the walls in the bathroom and bedroom. A rendering of Alessandro Mendini's famous Proust armchair faces the bed. Above it, and in contrast to the bright color scheme, hangs an ethereal painting of androgynous-looking women by Spanish artist Begonia Montalban. Though the rest of the bedroom décor forgoes the Technicolor levity of the living room for a more muted scheme, the tessellated wooden floor and modish creamsicle-colored bedspread are far from boring.

In the Presidential Suite, designer Alessandro Mendini shrugs off the sleek, understated aesthetic of Byblos's five-star competitors. Taking a few design cues from Philippe Starck, who created some of the furniture along with the likes of Ron Arad and Oscar Niemeyer, Mendini flanks an ornate stone fireplace with yellow-and-chrome wraparound chairs and a minimalist white table. Surrounded by see-through plastic scoop chairs, the dining table is similarly modern, despite the fact that it rests beneath a traditional chandelier and ceiling molding. The generously apportioned windows let in swathes of natural light, which gives the room an airy feeling.

Not content with simply dressing us, the Byblos brand has effectively lay claim to the latest lifestyle evolution: the luxury designer hotel. Byblos excels, however, by treating its guests as inhabitants of the art world, and not just as visitors passing through.

Byblos Art Hotel Villa Amista
Via Cedrare, 78
37029 Corrubbio di Negarine
Verona, Italy
T 39 045 6855555
F 39 045 6855500
www.byblosarthotel.com
info@byblosarthotel.com

Location
**Amstel,
the Netherlands**
Room
Suite Seven
Architect/Designer
Marcel Wanders
Rate
Expensive

INGENIOUSLY CONCEIVED
AND EXPERTLY EXECUTED,
THE HOTEL'S SIGNATURE STYLE
HAS INFLUENCED COUNTLESS
IMITATIONS.

LUTE SUITES

SEVEN TOWNHOUSES,
CONVERTED FROM AN
EIGHTEENTH-CENTURY
GUNPOWDER FACTORY,
MAKE UP THE HOTEL.

Designer Marcel Wanders and Dutch entrepreneur Peter Lute joined creative forces to forge a novel hotel experience at the Lute Suites in Ouderkerk aan de Amstel, located 20 minutes outside of Amsterdam and already a renowned destination among gastronomes for its inordinate number of world-class restaurants. Lute Suites bears little resemblance to a traditional hotel. Once a group of munitions factory buildings, these eighteenth-century townhouses have been converted into seven suites, each with its own entrance.

Wanders flexed his creative muscle in the jewel of the set: Suite Seven. The large duplex has an array of mostly black furniture set among the white walls, white floors, and white carpet that's punctuated by an occasional dash of color in the form of Miró-esque cushions and shaded lamps. But Wanders didn't entirely erase the old. The nuance of his touch is obvious in this airy suite's details, making it both inviting and comfortable. Clean geometric Bottoni sofas, upholstered in a fabric by Paul Smith, are offset by whorled chandeliers and sculptures that resemble large water-worn pebbles and whimsically protrude from the walls (pages 242 to 243). A teak spiral staircase leads to the sleeping area, where the floor is ornately patterned in a creative, steel-inlay twist on fleurs-de-lis (page 245). True to the tidy Dutch aesthetic, the bathroom is beautifully unadorned: A stark and rectangular bathtub faces orderly, curving wood slating and a baroque vanity and mirror (page 247). Red Bisazza mosaic tiles add subtle color (page 244, right).

The bathroom may be gorgeous, but the bedroom is inspiring. The walls are upholstered in dark, dimpled padding, and red, white, and gold lamps angled askance are playful touches in an otherwise spare room (page 244, left). Dark brown wood, metallic grays, and black are a restful contrast to the whitewashed splendor of the lower floor. But not to worry–the sunlight surging through the window keeps the space light.

While not extravagant, Suite Seven is fitted with many amenities, including all manner of electronics and a fully equipped kitchen. These aspects, combined with the loftiness of the place, cause it to resemble an expat's über-pad more than a whirlwind traveler's crashing place, and make it a perfect base to explore the rest of the Netherlands.

Special feature

The Lute Suite's riverboat. One of the Lute chefs can prepare lunch or dinner, while guests set sail on a tour of the river, Monday through Friday. On Saturdays, the hotel serves a special menu for the suite guests onboard the boat.

Can't miss

The food. It's a little known fact that the Lute Suites started as a restaurant, and for good reason. The Lute Restaurant, located in an old gunpowder factory next to the suites, is well worth a visit– don't pass up the tuna with wasabi marshmallows.

Lute Suites
Amsteldijk Zuid 54-58
1184 VD
Ouderkerk a/d Amstel
Amsterdam, The Netherlands
T 31 (0) 20 47 22 462
F 31 (0) 20 47 22 463
www.lutesuites.com
info@lutesuites.com

FILLED WITH THE COMFORTS
OF A WELL-HEELED HOME,
THE SUITE FEELS MORE
LIKE AN EXPAT'S ÜBER-PAD
THAN A HOTEL.

Location
**Barcelona,
Spain**
Room
Suite #516
Architect/Designer
Lázaro Rosa Violán
Rate
Expensive

EVERY ITEM HAS BEEN
HAND-CHOSEN BY
ITS DESIGNER, GIVING
THESE ROOMS A DISTINCT
LOOK THAT FEELS
COMFORTABLY TAILORED.

HOTEL
PULITZER

THE TERRACE OVERLOOKS
BARCELONA'S MOST
FAMOUS TOURIST SITES,
ALL WITHIN A SHORT
WALKING DISTANCE.

THE DESIGNER CHOSE
THE ART PIECES AND
EVEN TOOK SOME OF
THE PHOTOS HANGING
ON THE WALL.

Characterized by its great location just minutes from Plaza Catalunya, the Ramblas, and Paseo de Gracis–Hotel Pulitzer is turning heads for its stylish design features and charming ambiance. Interior designer Lázaro Rosa Violán's goal was to set about creating a hotel that felt more like a palace than a hotel–no small task in a city known for its design savvy. Radiating cosmopolitan cool, the hotel lobby evokes grandeur and beauty with its Sicilian altar-cum-reception desk. Every public area is flooded with natural light, which heightens the sense of spaciousness.

Outfitted with a terrace/solarium, Suite 516 is gracious in size and beautifully appointed. Violán favored inky blacks, pearly whites, and charcoal grays, but the sober color scheme gets a jolt of glitz with gold highlights, white leather, and caramel-toned wood detailing. Leather chairs flank the fireplace, lending a masculine touch to the room that contrasts with the canopied bed, which seemingly floats in the room (pages 248 to 249).

Even the bathroom is regal in size and pleasantly somber in its color palette (page 252). Art pieces like a Grecian-inspired sculpture and a framed purple-and-white kimono span the globe, from Europe to the Far East, and lend an exotic atmosphere to the otherwise subtle design Even the room's photos were chosen–and in some cases taken–by Violán, giving guests the feeling of staying in the guestroom at the designer's home.

The hotel is situated within walking distance to some of Barcelona's most popular tourist sites, like the Gothic Quarter, the Picasso museum, and Gaudí's house for the Battló family. A tourist destination in its own right, Hotel Pulitzer has enough panache to charm the most cynical of critics.

Special feature
Rooftop bar. Get a bird's-eye view on the surrounding area while sipping sangria.

Can't miss
The Visit. The hotel's premier restaurant combines Mediterranean cuisine with subtle Asian accents.

Hotel Pulitzer
C/ Bergera, 8
08002 Barcelona, Spain
T 34 934 81 67 67
www.hotelpulitzer.es
info@hotelpulitzer.es

Location
**Granada,
Spain**
Room
Presidential Suite
Architect/Designer
Hospes Design Team
Rate
Expensive

WITNESSING THE
ARCHITECTURAL STRUCTURE
OF THESE HOTELS IS WORTH
THE TRIP ALONE.

HOSPES
PALACIO

Converted from a nineteenth-century palace, Hospes Palacio de los Patos is a daring combination of two radically different buildings. The sculpturally voluptuous original structure was the home of a sugar cane magnate, while the new building favors clean, straight lines. When the Hospes Design Team undertook the renovation of the hotel, its main objective was to create a complex that was a well-balanced whole—a combination of the old world and the new world (page 257). To achieve that, the designers surrounded the hotel with a garden of palm trees and fragrant magnolias that frame a fountain with two swans, the namesake of the palace.

Special feature
The chocolate body massage at the hotel's Bodyna Spa & Wellness.

Can't miss
The Senzone Restaurant. Located on the ground floor of the new building, the restaurant is a transparent space, and guests can see the hotel's gardens through the glass walls. Teatime is served daily at five o'clock.

All 42 rooms—20 in the palace, 22 in the new building—have their own hallmark. Some preserve traces of the past, such as the elegant Presidential Suite with its plastered relief ceiling (pages 254 to 255). The color scheme is subdued, yet elegant: Black or white furniture, silver curtains and carpets, and purple chaise-lounges. From the suite's terrace, guests can sit and get a stunning view of the city's main shopping center, dotted with specialty boutiques, cafés, and fine restaurants. At the start of each visit, the hotel provides a welcome package that can include anything from a bottle of cava to an individually tailored spa package. In the Palacio de los Patos, guests discover luxury the old-fashioned way.

Hospes Palacio de los Patos
Solarillo de Gracia, 1
18002 Granada, Spain
T 34 958 535 790
F 34 958 536 968
www.hospes.es
hospes.palaciopatos@hospes.es

EACH GUEST GETS A WELCOME
PACKAGE THAT CAN INCLUDE
ANYTHING FROM A BOTTLE OF
CAVA TO A SPA TREATMENT.

Location
Madrid,
Spain
Room
First and eighth floor rooms
Architect/Designer
Zaha Hadid (first floor)
and Kathryn Findlay (eighth)
Rate
Expensive

THIS HOTEL IS A MASSIVE DESIGN ACHIEVEMENT, ONE THAT CASTS A LONG SHADOW ON HOTELIERS AND DESIGNERS ALL AROUND THE WORLD.

HOTEL PUERTA AMERICA

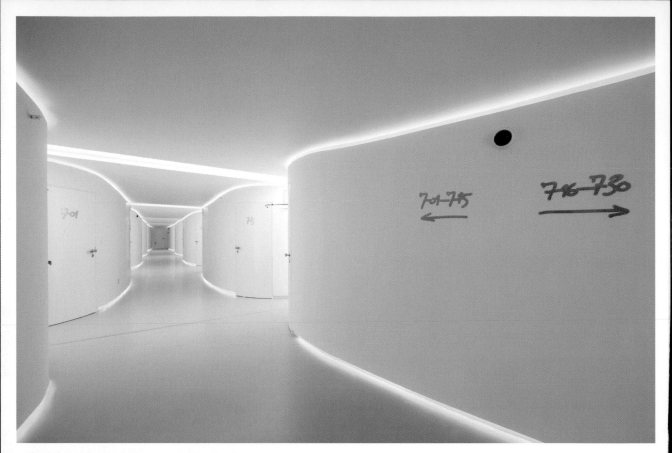

INSTEAD OF STANDOUT
ROOMS THERE ARE
COOL FLOORS—13
OF THEM, EACH ONE
RADICALLY DIFFERENT
FROM THE NEXT.

STYLE HAS NEVER
BEEN SO SLEEK OR
OUT OF THIS WORLD.

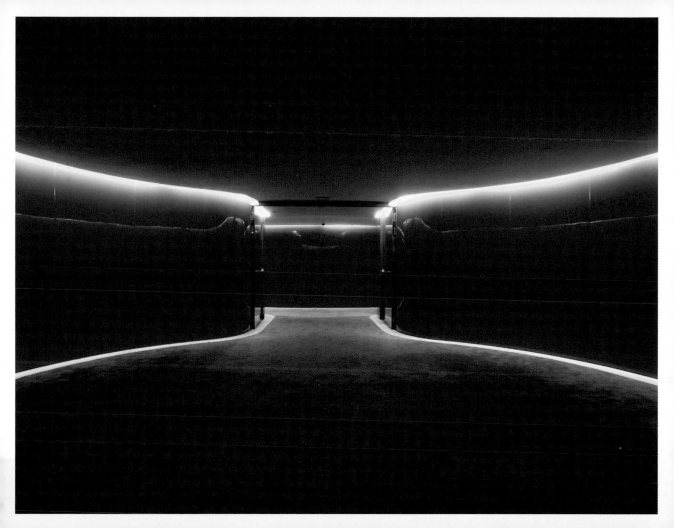

FUTURISTIC AND PLAYFUL, THE DESIGN IS OUT OF THE JETSONS.

To say that Hotel Puerta America is a radical design hotel would be an understatement. The 342-room hotel commissioned a different architect/interior designer of international standing to create each floor and the public spaces. This was not a collaborative effort. Each floor realizes the unique vision of the designer—from the elevator banks down to the blankets and bathrobes. The hotel has become a destination site itself.

The hotel's façade is covered with a rainbow of vinyl panels, which are actually a series of window screens to regulate the incoming light. When they unfold, the screens reveal phrases from Paul Eluard's poem, "Poésie et Vérité," written in all the major languages. Glass cube elevators slide up and down the exterior. At each floor, the doors open to reveal a new world. Although it's impossible to pick a standout room, the coolest floors are the first floor, designed by Zaha Hadid, and the eighth floor, designed by Kathryn Findlay.

Zaha Hadid—the first woman to win a Pritzker Prize, the Nobel of architecture—is noted for her use of fluid lines and at Hotel Puerta America, she utilizes this aesthetic to full effect. Hadid's mostly white-on-white and black-on-black guestrooms appear to be otherwordly (pages 258 to 259, 260 bottom right, and 263). There are no corners in the rooms; every surface is made of a molded Corian-like stone, and the rooms' sinuous, curved composition creates the bed, desk, and other furnishings into a single

sculpture enhanced by skillfully hidden lamps. Unique to the Hadid rooms are the bathrooms, which have a pleasant cavelike ambience, complete with a curved ceiling. While standing at the foot of the bathtub, it's nearly impossible to see where it ends and the sink countertop begins. The futuristic design conjures images of *The Jetsons* home: sleek, stylish, and playfully sophisticated. Even though Hadid's rooms lack the views of, say, the twelfth floor, they set the standard of excellence for the rest of the building.

Scottish architect Kathryn Findlay collaborated with lighting designer Jason Bruges to create the guestrooms on the eighth floor. Rather than using walls to designate separate spaces, Findlay employed barely there white curtains, which not only make the rooms feel larger and airy but also peacefully serene. The Findlay/Bruges experience begins the moment guests exit the elevator (261). Optical fiber panels on the wall trace guests' movements and construct new images with every additional movement. Within the rooms themselves, the bed is suspended from the floor to enhance the idea that guests are sleeping on a cloud. The bed's headboard functions as a desk, too. In the bathrooms, the shower cascades from the ceiling. The overall result is a dreamy environment, a space that promotes meditative moments.

None of the floors are even remotely similar. Chances are if these rooms don't fit the bill, one of the rooms on the other floors will.

Special feature

Pulling a switcheroo. Guests can change to a different floor each night at an additional charge of $74 per room change on floors like those created by Ron Arad (page 260, top and bottom left) and Marc Newson (page 263).

Can't miss

The tour. Can't spring for the room change? Go on a brief guided tour of the hotel by the management; it really is more of an art museum than a typical hotel.

Hotel Puerta America
Avenida de América, 41
28002 Madrid, Spain
T 34 917 445 400
F 34 917 445 401
www.hoteles-silken.com/
hpam/index.php

Location
**Stockholm,
Sweden**
Room
**The Green Room
with Greta Garbo**
Architect
**Bergkrantz
Arkitekter AB**
Designer
**Ahlgren Edblom
Arkitekter AB**
Rate
Moderate

A HOTEL THAT PAYS
HOMAGE TO THE WORLDS
OF ART, MUSIC, AND FILM,
MAKING IT A HIT AMONG
BUDDING AUTEURS
AND WOULD-BE DIVAS.

HOTEL
RIVAL

Originally opened in 1937 as the Aston Hotel, Hotel Rival was reinvented by owner Benny Andersson (former band member of Abba) in 2003. Included on-site with the hotel is a first-class bakery, café, bistro, and a cinema—one of Stockholm's best. In tribute to the latter, every one of the 99 guestrooms is decorated with scenes from well-known Swedish films. There's also an original 1940s cocktail bar with a modern dance floor and DJs on weekends. It's the perfect place for any dancing queen to watch the scene.

Special feature

The special pillow menu. Offering everything from duck down to buckwheat and natural fibers, this menu guarantees sweet dreams. If the pillow doesn't calm, there's also a Debenhams's teddy bear—one rests atop every bed.

Can't miss

The Rival Cinema. What other hotel can boast an in-house art deco movie theater in its basement? There's never been a better place for a Garbo retrospective.

Located on the east side of a public square off of Söder's busy Hornsgatan, the Rival is quintessentially Swedish in the sense that the interior design is highly functional—and looks good, too. Though every room has its own quirky personality, who can resist Greta Garbo? Awash in deep green bedding, the room is pleasantly simple; a stellar photo of Garbo hangs above the bed (pages 266 to 267)

Equipped with the usual hotel amenities—wall-mounted flat-screen TVs, great room service, and plush towels—it's the little details that give the room star power (page 269). Take the minibar, for instance. Not only is it well stocked but it's also at shoulder level rather than shin height, further evidence that you don't have to be a movie star to enjoy the good life.

Hotel Rival
Mariatorget 3
Box 175 25
SE-118 91 Stockholm, Sweden
T 46 08 545 789 00
F 46 08 545 789 24
www.rival.se

SCENES FROM
A SWEDISH MOVIE
DECORATE EACH
ROOM OF THE HOTEL,
WHICH IS OWNED BY
A FORMER MEMBER
OF ABBA.

Location
**Les Giettes,
Switzerland**
Room
Pavilion Pod
Architect/Designer
Sofia de Meyer
Rate
Expensive

WHITEPOD PROVIDES
A RARE OPPORTUNITY
FOR GUESTS TO
COMMUNE WITH
NATURE—6,000 FEET UP.

WHITE
POD

GUESTS ARE TREATED
TO BEDSIDE MASSAGES
IN THIS ECO-FRIENDLY,
COMFORTABLY
INSULATED TENT.

Committed to a zero-impact experience to ensure that nature and wildlife are protected, Whitepod provides a high-tech eco-camp for up to 24 guests. Located at an altitude of nearly 6,000 feet in the Swiss Alps, the journey from Lake Geneva starts with a taxi ride through breathtaking scenery of vineyards and farms to the village of Les Cerniers, where guests board a train that takes them to the edge of Whitepod's private ski run. Food is provided before the guide leads intrepid guests on a 20-minute hike to the alpine chalet-style farmhouse next to five geodesic-dome tents.

There are three different types of pods to choose from–Expedition, Pavilion, and Group. Unless there's an entire entourage traveling, in which case snag the Group pod, the Pavilion (pages 270 to 271) is the way to go–since it is equipped with a bathroom on-site, unlike the Expedition pods. Covered with white or green canvas depending on the season, the 8-foot-high pods blend perfectly into the surrounding landscape (page 272, bottom). Pitched on raised wooden platforms, the pods can be taken down at any time without leaving a trace of their existence; the frames are built to withstand heavy snowfalls and high winds. While each pod has a front terrace with an unobstructed view of the surrounding Alps, the Pavilion pod also has a mezzanine just beneath the skylight.

Special feature
Champagne fondue. Besides the fondue, dinners feature locally purchased food served at a candle-lit table. The local wines are excellent, too.

Can't miss
The views of the east face of Mont Blanc, the tallest peak in the Alps.

Lit by oil lamps and heated by wood stoves, each pod is insulated to maintain a comfortable indoor temperature and is surprisingly spacious inside (page 272, top). Each is furnished with fleamarket finds–an armchair and bleached pine vanity–as well as a full-size bed with sheepskin rugs and organic bedding. Natural light spills through the wide clear-vinyl front window. The pods come equipped with an iPod that has tunes ranging from Britpop to Barry White, but only Pavilion guests are treated to in-pod massages and treatments.

The renovated nineteenth-century alpine chalet next to the pods houses the main dining room, bar, and bathrooms, including a sauna. Whitepod is committed to recycling all waste generated by the camp.

With global warming threatening the snow pack of resorts at lower elevations, these eco-friendly pods stand at the forefront of the "green skiing" movement–though they're great for snowshoeing and tours on foot or dog-sled, too.

Although Whitepod has no limo, no bellman, and no electricity, with its incredible views of the majestic Alps and the unspoiled wilderness, it provides the ultimate mountain adventure.

Whitepod
Les Cerniers
Batt. Postale 681
1871 Les Giettes, Switzerland
T 41 24 471 3838
www.whitepod.com

Location
**United Kingdom,
Isle of Jura**
Room
White Room
Architect/Designer
Bambi Sloan
Rate
Expensive

THE COMFY AMBIANCE AT THE LODGE MAKES IT THE PERFECT PLACE TO ENJOY A NIGHTCAP OR TWO FROM THE LOCAL WHISKEY DISTILLERY.

JURA LODGE

CLEAN, AIRY, AND FULL OF LIGHT, THE WHITE ROOM IS PLEASANTLY UNCLUTTERED.

THE SLOGAN HERE IS
"NO PLASTIC!" INSTEAD,
THERE ARE UNIQUE FLEA
MARKET TREASURES.

With its desert-of-the-north topography of windswept bare hills, cliffs, and open fields, Jura is home to a rustic, no-nonsense kind of beauty. It is an unpretentious place where visitors can disappear into the countryside to cozy up at a pub with a dram of whiskey.

As one of the most remote and least inhabited places in Scotland, Jura is home to an award-winning whiskey distillery and an idyllic five-bedroom lodge, making it an exclusive retreat for true whiskey aficionados. (The lodge can only be rented out as a whole and guests either cook or bring a chef.) But the whiskey isn't the only draw. With stunning interiors designed by Parisian Bambi Sloan, Jura Lodge captures the spirit of the island, where the rugged meets the twee. Sloan uncovered one-of-a-kind treasures from French and Belgian flea markets, and scoured Spanish emporia for delicate vintage linens, lace, glass, and other accessories to complement more daring finds, like the antlers of African elk, gazelles, and antelope (pages 274 to 275, 279, and 281). Mixed in among the electric country décor is an old-fashioned refrigerator (page 278). The Bakelite telephones and ostrich-egg lamp stands are a reminder of Sloan's slogan, "No plastic!"

Special feature

The brew. An on-site nearly 200-year-old distillery offers single malts that range in age from 10 to 21 years old.

Can't miss

The Jura whiskey festival, which takes place every May, and the Jura Gardens, an exotic space cultivated by renowned gardener Peter Cool.

While every room in the lodge boasts Sloan's idiosyncratic style, the White Room is by far the best (pages 276 to 277). Featuring white walls, cream fretwork headboard, and calico drapes framing harbor views, "it's as good as life used to be," as the locals would say. The focal point of the room is its free-standing, claw-footed roll-top bath, perfectly positioned for a view of the sea. The soaking tub supports Sloan's claim that the White Room isn't so much of a bedroom but a "big bathroom with a bed." Sloan's unashamedly romantic vision of the Scottish beach house heralds a return to the simple pleasures of life: enjoying a long bath, eating locally caught lobster, and sharing a rare single malt by the fireside with friends and family.

As the lodge's proprietors say, there is no quick way of getting to the island. The fastest method from London involves two planes, a ferry, and the best part of day. George Orwell, who stayed here to write *1984*, was attracted by its reclusive nature, and it still appeals to writers and others looking for a quiet refuge.

Jura Lodge may be hard to get to but as those who've been there will testify, it's a place that's even harder to leave.

Jura Lodge
Isle of Jura Distillery
Craighouse, Isle of Jura,
Argyll PA60 7XT
T 0496 820240
F 0496 820344
www.isleofjura.com/lodge
info@isleofjura.com

GEORGE ORWELL,
WHO WROTE 1984
HERE, CALLED IT AN
"UN-GETTABLE PLACE."

Location
United Kingdom,
London
Room
Rooftop Studio Deluxe
Architect
Chetwood Associates
Designer
Precious McBane
Rate
Expensive

NOTHING COULD BE
BETTER THAN THE
ZETTER, A HOTEL THAT
APPEALS TO THE TRAVEL-
SAVVY PARTY-GOER.

THE
ZETTER

GUESTS CAN STEP OUT
ONTO THE DECK AND
GAZE OUT AT THE LONDON
SKYLINE, OR PARTAKE
OF THE LIBRARY'S 4,000
DIGITAL MUSIC TRACKS.

The 59-guestroom Zetter, a former Victorian warehouse on Clerkenwell Road in London's increasingly trendy Farringdon, showcases eco-friendly design without being self-righteous. Natural light floods down from the five-story, semielliptical atrium onto a spiraling staircase and elevators decorated in a red-mirrored boudoir theme. A borehole drilled beneath the property provides water, which is purified and bottled for drinking. When a window is opened, the air conditioning automatically turns off.

The cutting-edge design, with unplastered walls and "floating" ceilings, is a clever mix of the modern and the traditional. Secondhand furniture mingles with classical pieces. A flamboyant chandelier of pink glass lilies dominates the simple, tiny lobby. Artwork and handicrafts from local artisans stand beside vintage Wegner and Prouve and bespoke wallpaper by Eley Kishimoto and Timorous Beasties.

In the Rooftop Studio Deluxe on the fifth floor, floor-to-ceiling windows open onto an enormous wood deck that matches the room in size and displays a view of London's skyline (page 284). The soft furnishings and ambient, pink-tinted mood lighting create an adult backdrop for an array of entertainment, which includes an eclectic mix of original Penguin classics, wide-screen TV, and access to 4,000 digital music tracks (pages 282 to 283). The eco-theme reemerges in the bathroom with the rainfall shower and natural bath products.

In the hotel's fashionable, youthful, and eclectic ambiance another surprise is the good value for the money, making this hotel a true trend-Zetter.

Special Feature

The vending machines. Instead of the standard hotel minibar, vending machines in the corridors dispense a wide array of products and beverages, ranging from champagne and cappuccino to disposable cameras and toothpaste.

Can't miss

The Mediterranean dishes. The Zetter Restaurant, on the ground floor, serves such delicious fare as tomato, fennel, and mussel soup and grilled mushroom and asparagus salad. Its floor-to-ceiling windows create a bright, airy space that overlooks an adjoining square.

The Zetter
St John's Square
86-88 Clerkenwell Road
London EC1M 5RJ
United Kingdom
T 44 (0)20 7324 4444
F 44 (0)20 7324 4445
www.thezetter.com
info@thezetter.com